THE WAR IS OVER BUT CHILDREN STILL HAVE QUESTIONS

DAVID STOOP, Ph.D.
Minirth-Meier-Stoop Clinic
STEPHEN ARTERBURN, M.Ed.
New Life Treatment Centers, Inc.

Tyndale House Publishers, Inc.
Wheaton, Illinois

Front cover photos copyright © 1991
Comstock and Dave DeJong

ACKNOWLEDGEMENTS

Our thanks to those who helped us find the hearts
of our children and the fears that needed to be
calmed. Connie Neal, Linda Christeson, Katie
Temple, and Margaret Snyder all went into high
gear to help us meet a tough deadline.

Our special thanks to the students of Stoneybrook
Christian Elementary School, whose questions are
found within these pages.

—Dave Stoop and Stephen Arterburn

96 95 94 93 92 91
7   6   5   4   3   2   1

*Dedicated to the families of
those who lost loved ones
in the Persian Gulf.
Thank you for your sacrifice.*

CONTENTS

HOW TO TALK TO YOUR KIDS ABOUT WAR AND PEACE

A three-year-old boy walked into his preschool and asked his teacher, "How's Joe?" The teacher didn't know anyone named Joe, so she asked whom he was talking about. The boy replied, "You know — G.I. Joe and his friends! The ones over there fighting."

The teacher was surprised he knew about the war. She asked how he knew about G.I. Joe and his friends. "Oh, I know all about the war," he said. "My eight-year-old brother told me everything."

War affects children, especially with the advent of the "television war." The recent Persian Gulf War — as TV reported the fighting and bombing from Baghdad — made many parents suddenly aware of the impact of war on their children.

Through television, war is no longer remote or abstract. It is real, and it comes into our houses.

Some young children have actually been worried about bombs or missiles being launched into their house through the television set. As absurd as it might seem to an adult, this can be a serious and real concern to a child. We need to understand how to answer questions and fears such as these.

Many of us think that our children consider war to be like one of the video games they play. The pictures taken by the TV camera in the nose of a missile or in a "smart bomb" look like the pictures children see when they play video games. But other TV images of devastation overcome the video game effect upon kids. The constant urgency of news bulletins on TV make war very real indeed to children young and old.

In the aftermath of war, children's questions don't stop, and studies show that war's effects on children don't end either. Children are still concerned about what happened and whether war might start up again. As soldiers return home to parades and celebrations, children want to know what is happening. One elementary- school child's question had to do with military holidays such as Veterans Day and the Fourth of July: "Why do we celebrate war?" she wanted to know.

Even after a war ends, it will be remembered by your child. It may become a negative memory of a scary time, or it may become a positive image that will prompt him to embrace new heroes. In any case, war is a time when children ask deep questions of themselves and of their parents, and it's important that they be given helpful, honest, comforting answers.

What should you say to your child about war? The answer depends on the age of the child. Younger children, ages three to five, will not understand technical or rational explanations. What they do want is for you to take their question seriously. What they are looking for is the loving reassurance that you are not going to let anything bad happen to them.

With older children, ages six to twelve, it is important for you to help them sort out what is real. Parents need to help these children express the uncomfortable emotions they feel inside. Children have very active imaginations; as adults, we may forget how those imaginations can overwhelm a child.

With children of any age, it is essential to be honest and forthright. Encourage your child to talk about war. Children know when adults are not telling the truth — they have built-in honesty detectors! They can see through a faked answer or a dodge to their questions. They can feel a parent's own uneasiness about war.

At the same time it is possible for parents to provide too much information, or give information children have no interest in. As a parent, you are your child's filter. Your task — a difficult one — is to communicate the truth in bite-sized morsels that your child can easily digest.

Certainly, television viewing of war needs to be monitored by parents. This is just as true after a war as during — in fact in the aftermath of war, images displayed on the TV screen can be even more graphic, as reporters and cameras suddenly have access to the battlefield. Remember that there is no R-rating for news — especially war news. Some news reports from the battlefield go on air without previewing or editing. Some commentators now warn the viewing audience that what will be shown next could be upsetting to children. Pay attention to these warnings and monitor what the TV networks are presenting to your kids.

Detecting Danger Signals

While war affects all children to a degree, it seems to influence certain children more deeply. Some warning signs of a more serious problem are:

• Persistent fears about war that interfere with a child's regular activities; ongoing fears that war might start up again

- Sleep changes—restless sleep, nightmares, awakening in the middle of the night—that persist for several weeks
- Changes in the way a child eats that persist beyond several days
- Changes in a child's ability to concentrate
- Prolonged increase in irritability
- Atypical behavior problems at school or home
- Declining grades and performance in class
- Physical complaints—stomachaches, headaches, dizziness—when there are no other symptoms of illness
- An increase in a child's negative talk about himself or others
- Withdrawal from friends and from family

Some changes in your child's behavior may be signals but are also healthy ways for him to cope. A young child may cling to a favorite toy or blanket, or want to cling to you. Don't become irritated by this behavior—see it as evidence that your child is having trouble dealing with the realities of war, and then try to talk with him about what both you both are feeling.

The hidden issue behind any change in your child during or after a war is one of trust. Your child is really asking, "Can I still trust you?"

"Will you be there for me?" "Are you taking care of me?" "Can I depend on you?" You need to be close to your child so that he knows he can continue to trust you for his safety and security.

What Can Be Learned from War?

War can be an opportunity to teach your child values about life. There are many parallels between countries at war and children fighting on the playground. War is about right and wrong, rules being observed or broken, friends and enemies.

War is a conflict. All of us experience conflict in our daily lives — this includes our children. In the conflicts faced by your child, rules are very important. Children have an innate sense of justice — "It's not fair!" is their constant cry. Telling them that life is not fair does not satisfy that need, even though the statement is true. A child needs to learn that truth from experience, and your talking to him about fairness and justice in the way wars are conducted will help satisfy that need within.

Answering questions about war can give you a chance to express to your own child thoughts about peace and peacemaking. "When is it right to fight?" "When should we turn the other cheek?" "What is a pacifist?" "Why did people protest the war?" All of these questions represent opportunities for you to instill values in your child and to teach him about making responsible choices.

War also teaches a child about spiritual things. During and immediately after wartime a child thinks about prayer in a new way. It changes from a rote activity into a comforting time before bed at night. Children think about God more during a time of crisis, and that becomes an opportunity for you to talk to your child about Jesus and to read the Bible together.

Perhaps we shouldn't forget that as adults we can learn from our own children's questions about war. Children have a way of expressing feelings in remarkably uncluttered ways. Sometimes their simple questions are quite profound and cause us to think more carefully about matters we might otherwise take for granted. "How does the enemy feel?" one child asked.

Using This Book

The questions in this book were collected from children in several elementary schools. We especially want to thank Margaret Snyder and all the children at Stoneybrook Elementary School in Dana Point, California, for taking the time to write out their questions for us.

The answers to the questions are aimed at children between the ages of six and twelve. The answers are written so you can read them to your child. If you prefer, put the answer into your own words. Some answers carry an additional suggestion that is more appropriate for your preschool child.

You will also find "Notes to Parents" in the answer to some questions. This is additional information for your own understanding about your child during and after war. It may help you provide a better, deeper answer to your child's question.

Dealing with your children's questions about war and peace is not a one-time thing. A story was told of a father who thought he had explained everything about the war to his son. The father had explained to his son that the range of the SCUD missile was the same as the distance from San Francisco to Los Angeles. The boy had learned the differences in time zones between the United States and Baghdad. Seemingly adjusted to these facts about war, the boy settled into a routine that included watching the Disney Channel and playing Nintendo instead of watching TV programs interrupted by war reports.

But one day outside their house an old

Volkswagen sparked and backfired. Hearing the explosion, the boy broke into tears. He looked at his father and asked, "Daddy, is the war coming?" Obviously, the fears and anxiety of this young boy went beyond his knowledge of specific facts about the war. He needed to turn to his father for comfort.

As you answer your children's questions about war, keep in mind what your children need most—the comfort and security that can come only from you.

CHAPTER 1

Questions about War

1 What is war?

When two or more people are angry and hurt each other, it is called a fight. When two countries, or even more than two countries, are angry and try to hurt each other, it is called war. War is fought when countries disagree and can't work out their problems by talking together.

Often, wars are fought because one country wants some or all of the land that another country has. If it wants the land badly enough, it will fight to try to win it. Sometimes when other countries see this happening, they might get into the war to protect the country who wants to keep its land.

Think about the war like you think about your friends and enemies. If a big bully tried to take away your friend's dog, you might decide to help your friend save his dog. You would team up with your friend against the big bully.

This is how countries, large and small, come together to protect each other. It is called "forming an alliance." When groups of countries, or alliances, fight, it is sometimes called a world war. So many countries are angry with each other that it seems like the whole world is fighting.

War is never a very good thing because some people get hurt, some people are killed, and it all costs a lot of money. But sometimes wars have to be fought because we want to protect ourselves, and we want to protect others from the bullies that sometimes are in charge of countries.

An example of this is the war that was fought in the Persian Gulf. Saddam Hussein, the president of Iraq, also wanted to be president of the land of Kuwait. He liked that land because it had many oil wells that made money and because a lot of the country is next to the sea, which makes it easy to ship the oil to other countries. One day he sent his army into Kuwait and took over the whole country. He killed many people, and said that Kuwait was now a part of Iraq. The United States is friends with Kuwait, and we formed an alliance with other countries like England, France, and Saudi Arabia to get Saddam Hussein's army out of Kuwait. This was so we could give the country back to the people of Kuwait, who were in charge of it before the war.

We did not want to go to war with Iraq. We had nothing against the people there. But we could not allow Saddam Hussein to be mean to all the people in Kuwait. We talked to him and gave him many chances to send his army back home. We told him it was wrong to take over another country and hurt its people. When he refused to listen to us, we met again with the other countries in our alliance. Together we decided if Saddam Hussein did not leave Kuwait, we would try to force him out. This is not always the best way, but it was the only way the alliance felt it could get Iraq's army out of Kuwait. So when Saddam Hussein still refused to leave Kuwait, we started to drop bombs on his army in Kuwait and also on his army and weapons in Iraq. We were not trying to bomb the people of Iraq, just the army. After a lot of bombing, we finally forced Saddam Hussein out of Kuwait. The bombing wasn't something we wanted to do, but we did it to help our friends. We also fought the war because we wanted to teach other countries the lesson that you cannot take over another country just because you feel like it. It is not fair.

Sometimes wars do not occur between two countries. They take place between groups of people inside a country that have a different set of beliefs or ideas. In the United States, we had a war called the Civil War. Some thought that people should have slaves, and some thought they should not. Those who wanted slaves wanted to form a new country where it would be OK to own slaves. A war had to be fought to keep the country together. Otherwise the United States would now be two countries instead of just one. Other countries have these kinds of civil wars for other reasons. If they do not like their leader, and if he will not give up his position, others fight a war to remove him as the leader.

War is a tragic thing in our world. It is always better to talk things over than fight things out. But as long as the world has existed, there have been wars and there will always be wars. We need to work together to bring peace to the world and prevent as many wars as possible.

2 Do innocent people die in a war?

In any war innocent people are often hurt and killed. Even in the worst country with the meanest army there will be innocent soldiers who do not want to be fighting. Sometimes they fight just so their own leaders won't kill them. They get killed fighting for something they don't even believe in. Many Americans died in the Vietnam War who did not think it was right for us to be fighting in Vietnam. They fought anyway because they loved America. Many of these innocent soldiers died. Often the most innocent people that die are the willing and dedicated soldiers in the war.

Sometimes people are killed who are not fighting the war. It is rarely done on purpose, but it does happen. Sometimes the computers that guide the bombs make a mistake. Instead of hitting a building with weapons or supplies in it, it hits a house or a neighborhood. Our country does everything it can to prevent killing women, children, and anyone who is not actually fighting.

There are some mean people who do kill innocent people on purpose. If they are caught when the war is over, they are punished for doing this. Killing innocent people is called a war crime. If someone is found guilty of doing it, that person might be put to death.

3 Do we bomb people's houses?
No, not on purpose.

When we bomb another country, we are aiming at targets that are part of the other country's army, air force, or navy. A military target is a building that has something in it that helps the enemy fight the war. It might be a big airplane hangar with fighter jets or bombers in it. It could have radar equipment that tries to track our planes as they fly. These are the types of targets that we try to bomb in a war.

But sometimes a bomb will drop from one of our planes and hit other buildings by mistake. In every recent war, some bombs have been dropped on houses. This is called civilian bombing. It is a terrible tragedy of war. Any time we find out we have bombed someone's house, we change the direction we are firing missiles or dropping bombs.

4 What is friendly fire?

When a soldier sees or hears bombs explode on the battlefield, he knows it is either enemy fire or friendly fire. "Enemy fire" means bombs that come from the enemy. "Friendly fire" means bombs that come from the soldier's own army.

The term "friendly fire" is often used when our own soldiers are injured or killed from our own bullets or bombs. If we try to bomb or shoot at an enemy and end up hitting our own people, we say it was a casualty resulting from friendly fire. This happens when soldiers do not talk to each other enough to know where their own army is and where the enemy is. It also happens when computers make mistakes and miscalculate where bombs should be dropped. Instead of bombs dropping on the enemy troops, they fall on our own friendly troops. From time to time friendly fire happens when one of our soldiers stands up in front of another of our soldiers and is hit by the bullet.

There is nothing friendly about friendly fire. The term just means that a friend, not an enemy, has pulled the trigger accidentally.

In the Persian Gulf War there were seven soldiers that were killed in one friendly fire accident. A rocket hit the truck they were riding in. The rocket came from someone on our side.

5 How much does war cost, and who pays for it?

War costs a lot of money. How much it costs depends on how many soldiers are sent to fight and how many bullets are shot and how many bombs are dropped. Some say the Persian Gulf War cost one-half billion dollars a day. Some of the missiles we launched in that war cost a million dollars. Some of the airplanes that were shot down cost more than $100 million. Also, just providing enough food for all the soldiers is a huge expense.

Everyone in the country pays taxes to help pay

for the war. Certain amounts of money are taken from the taxes collected and are used to defend the country. Some of the money your mother or father earn from their work goes into taxes and is spent on the war. Some of the money will go to train the soldiers so they will know how to fight. Other money will be spent on equipment like guns and rockets so they will be able to fight when the war comes.

In addition to our own money, we sometimes get money from other countries to help us, especially when we defend their own country. Other countries may give money to pay us to fight because they don't have soldiers of their own. In the Persian Gulf War, Kuwait gave the United States billions of dollars because we defended their country. Other countries like Japan also gave us money to fight the war.

6 How many people die in a war?

Sometimes thousands die and sometimes hundreds of thousands die. It depends on how long the war lasts and how many bombs fall and how many bullets are shot on each side.

Even if only one person dies in war, it's one person too many. Sometimes a war is necessary, but even then it's a terrible thing when someone dies in that war. If someone you know or someone in the family dies, you come to understand how even one person dying is too many.

The following list will give you an idea of how many American people have died in the past wars:

Civil War 620,000
World War I 117,000
World War II 400,000
Korean War 54,000
Vietnam War 58,000

7 How does war start?

There are many ways that a war can start.

When a country decides to take over another country, it might surprise attack that country and start bombing or roll its tanks over the ground toward the soldiers. When the United States was in a war with Japan, it was a surprise attack by Japan that started the war. The Japanese air force flew to Hawaii and dropped bombs on many of our ships in a place called Pearl Harbor. Just after the bombs dropped, Franklin Roosevelt, the President of the United States back then, declared war on Japan. That declaration was the official start of the war.

When there is an argument between two

countries, often one country will set a deadline. A leader might say, "If the other country does not pull all of its soldiers out by noon tomorrow, we will begin fighting. If noon comes and the soldiers are still where they aren't supposed to be, the war would start.

8 What if you don't want to fight?

Not everyone involved in a war actually does the fighting. Some people work on things like radios in buildings far away from the fighting. Others take care of the wounded and serve as doctors, nurses, and medical assistants. All of these people are called support staff. Although they don't actually fight, they provide support for those who do fight.

A person who wants to serve the country but does not believe in war is called a conscientious objector. Anyone can declare they are a conscientious objector and not have to fight. They serve the country in what is called a non-combat role.

9 What makes something bomb-proof?

Something that is bomb-proof will not be destroyed if a bomb is dropped on it. Most buildings that are above the ground could be destroyed by a bomb and are not bomb-proof.

Bomb-proof places are usually deep in the ground, like a cellar, only much deeper. Many of these bomb-proof places are called bunkers. They are protected by thick layers of concrete and metal. On a normal house, a wall might be as thick as your arm. On a bomb-proof shelter a wall might be as thick as a whole house. It costs a lot of money to make something bomb-proof.

In our country, some of our military command centers are deep within mountains in order to make them bomb-proof. We do this so that the leaders in a war can stay alive in order to lead our country and our troops.

10 Is hurting people ever OK?

Some people say that hurting people is never OK. These people are called pacifists, and they believe that hurting someone is never right. This belief is often part of their religion, so it's what their church believes.

Many people, though, believe that sometimes we must hurt a person to stop him from hurting other people. They don't want to do this, but they think it's the only way to keep others from being hurt.

There are some people who like to hurt others. These bullies pick on people they think they can beat up. If a bully decided to hurt you, you would probably want someone else — maybe one of your friends — to stop the bully.

When big countries try to bully little countries, they hurt the little countries. Sometimes we have to hurt those who are in charge of the big bully countries just so they will leave other countries alone.

Hurting others is not a good thing, but sometimes it seems the only way to get someone to pay attention and stop the bad things they are doing. If you have ever had your hand slapped so you would not burn it on a stove or fire, you know what I mean when I say that sometimes it is OK to hurt a person. Sometimes you have to hurt them for their own good, and sometimes you have to hurt them for the good of others.

11 Will there be a draft?

The draft happens when we do not have enough soldiers to fight a war. Today all of our soldiers have volunteered to fight. They were not drafted like many of the soldiers that fought in other wars such as Vietnam.

Sometimes people worry about the draft because they are afraid Mom or Dad may be drafted and asked to go fight. When a draft happens, young people are drafted first. People between the ages of eighteen and twenty-four usually are drafted long before older people.

As of today we have plenty of volunteer soldiers to protect our country. We had plenty of soldiers to fight the recent Persian Gulf War. There is little chance of a draft being started anytime soon.

12 Why do we let women fight?

There are many women who join our military who want to fight the enemy in whatever way they can. Some are pilots of planes, and some fly helicopters. Others work computers and other machines that are needed to keep track of the enemy. For years our government did not want women to have an active role in the military. In the past women had to be nurses to help our country in wartime. Today people have changed their minds about what women should and shouldn't do in war. They have earned respect and the right to protect this country just as men do. In fact, some women have very dangerous jobs in the military. We should be very thankful we have so many dedicated women who are willing to protect this country.

13 How can we tell who is winning the war?

It is hard to tell who is winning a war. Part of the military might be doing very well while another part is having a hard time. Sometimes reporters think they have heard what has happened and later they find out the facts were different. The enemy often distorts what is going on to confuse us. Sometimes an enemy will lie to make his own soldiers think things are going better than they really are. War can be confusing.

Most people agree that the side of the war that is losing the most people and machines is the side that is losing. Another sign of losing is if the soldiers on one side are forced to turn around and go back in the direction they came from. If they have to retreat, back up, and lose ground, it is most likely they are losing.

Winning a war means that the enemy finally gives up or runs away. Everything in war is done to make one side finally give up and quit fighting. This is usually followed by both sides signing an agreement not to fight. This is called a treaty. The side who wins the war is allowed to write what the treaty will say.

14 What happens if we don't win a war?

The result of not winning is different with every war. In the Persian Gulf War, if we had not won, we would have had to allow Iraq to run Kuwait. We would have left the area feeling very sad because our soldiers would have died even though nothing good would have come from their being brave enough to die.

In the Persian Gulf War, losing would not have changed anything in the United States. Since we were fighting for another country, our own country would not have been hurt. We would have been sad and other countries might have been mad at us, but we would have been safe.

When we were at war with Japan in World War II, we could have lost our country if we had not won. That would have meant that other people would be running the country in Washington, D.C. In the Vietnam War, our country was not in danger.

15 What is it like to be a soldier?

Being a soldier is a tough job. Soldiers are hard workers who are brave enough to fight the enemy. If a soldier is in the army, he might sleep in a tent on the ground. He might have to dig a big hole and sleep in it. A soldier in the navy sleeps in a bunk bed on a ship.

The soldier on the ground sometimes goes for days without a shower. They go to the bathroom outside, not in a clean restroom with tile and mirrors. Their food comes out of cans and is sometimes dehydrated. Dehydrated food has all the water taken out so it is lighter to carry and will not become rotten. Soldiers have to add water to dehydrated food before they can eat it.

Sometimes there are surprises for soldiers. In the Persian Gulf War, the cooks made up trucks filled with hamburgers, and they drove to the soldiers on the battlefield to feed them hot hamburgers.

Soldiers spend many hours training to fight. When war happens, they may spend days waiting before fighting starts. Once it does, it can be scary. Deadly bombs and bullets come close to where the soldiers are. Soldiers must be smart and alert to stay alive. But even the smartest ones sometimes are hurt or killed because the enemy knows what kind of weapons to use and the right time to use them. It is important to remember that although it is a dangerous job, most people that go to fight do not get hurt. Most return home safely.

Most soldiers have one feeling in common. They want whatever war they are fighting to be over so they can come home. They miss their family and friends. They want to be back home. They hope and pray war will end quickly.

16 How do mines explode?

Mines are bombs buried in the ground or floating in the water. They go off in different ways. Most have a trigger or several triggers that go off when something touches them. If a soldier steps on a mine, the trigger goes off and the mine explodes. If a boat comes up against a mine floating in the water, the side of the boat will hit the trigger and cause an explosion. If a car or truck drives over a mine in the road, it will set off the trigger and blow up the mine.

Some mines are even trickier than those. They work on electronic signals. If a person or a truck goes by a sensor, it blows up the mine up ahead. Fortunately we have a lot of machines that blow up the mines before anyone is hurt by them. We drop bombs, use road graders and other things that prevent our soldiers from being blown up on the land. On the ocean we use special boats called mine sweepers that help clear the water so a boat can go through safely.

17 What are chemical bombs?

Chemical bombs are bombs that contain poisonous gas. When the bomb blows up, the gas is let into the air. Anyone who breathes the gas gets sick because it is poison. There aren't very many of these chemical bombs because the big countries in the world have agreed not to make them. But some leaders of other countries have these bombs, so our soldiers have to be extra careful.

We have made special suits for our soldiers that allow them to breathe when chemical bombs explode. These suits prevent many soldiers from being killed and hurt. Soldiers also carry medicine to make the poison go away if they breathe any of it in. Maybe one day all the nations will have given up using these terrible bombs that can hurt so many people.

18 How do bombs know where to go?

Many of our bombs are dropped out of the bottom of an airplane and fall to the ground. They do not know exactly where to go; they just explode wherever they happen to land.

Some modern bombs have computers inside them that guide them to the target. These are sometimes called "smart bombs." Some of these have a special computer map inside. When the bomb launcher makes a dot on that map with the computer, the bomb knows to find that place on the earth. Other bombs have a special device that searches for hot spots. Since tanks and airplanes have very hot engines, when the bomb is launched, it goes after the hot engines of those tanks and planes and blows them up.

19 How are prisoners treated?

A few years ago several countries got together in Europe and had a big meeting. Since the meeting was held in the city of Geneva, this big meeting was called the Geneva Convention.

The countries came together in this place to develop rules about war. They decided if we had to have wars, we should agree ahead of time about what is fair and what is not fair when fighting a war. The Geneva Convention created a number of war rules. Today during war, anyone who does something against these rules can be punished when the war is over. These people are called war criminals because they did not follow accepted rules of war.

One of the rules is that prisoners must be treated with respect. They should not be tortured, and they should be given food and a nice place to sleep. The bad thing is that some countries do not follow these rules. Although most prisoners are treated well, many are hurt by the enemy. Some are tortured cruelly. Fortunately all the leaders know the rules and most of them follow them, so usually our prisoners are not hurt.

20 How do soldiers killing each other in a war solve the world's problems?

Soldiers killing each other is a terrible way to have problems solved. The soldiers fight for the country so that everyone else in the country does not have to fight.

It is like a school that has a soccer team. If that team plays another soccer team and wins, it is like the whole school won. Really the school did not win the game — only the kids playing on the field won the game. But because they represent the whole school, their win stands for the win of the whole school.

That is how it works with soldiers and armies. We do not want little children or old people to have to fight in a war. We also only want those who have been trained to fight to be out there fighting. So instead of untrained people going to war, only the soldiers go. If they win, it is a win for the entire country.

21 What do soldiers wear?

Soldiers wear special uniforms designed to help them fight the war. The soldier on the ground wears heavy boots that keep feet warm and prevent them from being crushed. Their pants are of heavy material. They have pockets that hold what they need for fighting. There are special loops and hooks to latch things onto. Most wear a special belt that holds guns, water, bullets, and other items. Their helmets are of hard material that protects their heads in case a piece of metal from a bomb hits them.

When soldiers fight in the cold, they wear heavy jackets; when they fight in the heat, they wear cooler clothes. Everything they wear is designed especially for the work they do. It helps and protects them.

22 Where do they bury soldiers when they die?

Many soldiers are buried in national cemeteries that are reserved only for our war heroes. In Washington, D.C., Arlington National Cemetery is full of white crosses on the graves of our brave soldiers.

Sometimes soldiers write down where they

wish to be buried before they go and fight. Every soldier knows that death is a possibility, so they often make those kinds of arrangements just in case they do not come back alive.

CHAPTER 2

Questions about Feelings, Safety, and Security

23 Will bombs fall on my house?

No, we don't think so. Sometimes it is hard to
know how far away we are from a war. When on
TV we can see men fighting and airplanes
dropping bombs, we really don't know whether
they are close or far away. Usually, the war is far
away.

Note to parents: Television has made the world shrink into what has
been called a global village. Young children, especially, have no
concept of distance. "Far away" may mean as nearby as Grandma's
house. Use the map on page 159 of this book or a globe to show
your child where the war is. Show them where you live and then
show them where Grandma lives. Help them to see there are
different "far aways."

A question like this is often about deeper issues for the child.
Younger children may only need you to answer this question with a
no and then a hug and the reassurance that you love them and that
you will protect them.

Older children need the same reassurances but perhaps will
require more factual information. Keep in mind that the main point
of this question isn't distance — it is really about safety and
protection. The real question is "Will you protect me?"

24 Will my dad, or anyone in my family, have to go to war?

Some moms and dads have had to go to war. Do
you know anyone whose mom or dad has gone

to war? In our country, our armed forces are made up of volunteers. It hasn't always been that way and that isn't true in every country. Some countries have what is called a "draft." That means that you had to register with the government when you had your eighteenth birthday, and they could make you join the army, navy, air force, or marines, depending on who needs people. Our country used to have a draft, but we don't have a draft now, so no one has to join the military.

Members of your family will not have to go to war unless they have joined the military by choice. Even if they have joined, not everyone in the military goes to war. It depends on their job in the military. Some have to stay behind to get supplies and food to our soldiers. Others serve in different parts of the world from where the war is and need to stay where they are to do their job.

If one of your friends, parents, or family members had to go to war, it is because they have already joined the military. When they joined the military, they did so to serve our country and help protect it. Most really don't want to fight in a real war, and most don't have to. It's scary to have someone you love have to go to war. Nobody likes to be left behind and not be able to help out.

25 Do we need gas masks in our home?

No, we don't. Only those who live in countries close enough to a war need gas masks. And they need them only when one of the leaders of those fighting has chemical or biological weapons. Most countries in the world today have agreed not to use these kinds of weapons. Our country doesn't use them.

During the war in the Persian Gulf, the enemy leader, Saddam Hussein, threatened to use chemical and biological weapons. So people in countries near him, and our soldiers who were fighting him, needed gas masks. They were close enough that they needed protection.

26 If my parents get killed, who will take care of me?

Most parents, even those not involved in a war, have made arrangements for someone they know and trust to take care of their children in case something happened to them. They usually pick someone you know and love as well.

Note to parents: If you have made this kind of arrangement for your children, it would be helpful to talk to them and tell them whom you have picked. Then listen to their thoughts and feelings about your choice.

Abandonment is one of our greatest fears and is especially fearful to a child. It is reassuring to a child to know that other people

besides their parents love and care for them. Letting them know that
you have thought about this will be of great comfort.

27 Why don't I feel safe?

War always makes people feel unsafe. It is
natural for you to have these feelings. What you
need to know is that we feel some of the same
things. We family members need to take care of
each other.

Note to parents: Often children reflect the emotions of the family or
of their parents. If you are afraid, anxious, or nervous, your child
will pick up these feelings from you and experience them as if they
were their own feelings. The same is true of other adults in your
child's life. A teacher who is nervous or anxious about the war can
stir up these same feelings in your child.

It is important to ask your child what is making him or her feel
unsafe. There may be a specific question that is at the root of the
fear. Sometimes answering a specific question will take care of the
problem.

28 Will terrorists hurt me?

No, probably not. We hear a lot about what
terrorists might do, but their actions are limited.
We are afraid of terrorists because we don't
know what they will do, when they will do it, or
where they will do it. When terrorists do act,
they do things that are harmful and can hurt
people. So we need to know they are out there
and be careful.

Our country has a lot of people whose job it is

to make it safe for you and me. Part of their job is to catch terrorists before they do anything. That is why we have to go through metal detectors at the airport. The police are also being very careful about cars being left at an airport or someone leaving his suitcase unattended. This is part of how they are trying to make it safe for us.

It is the unknown that scares us. What terrorists will do is unknown to us. When we hear about a terrorist hijacking an airplane, we get afraid, and the hijacker gets a lot of attention in the news. But we don't hear anything about all of the thousands of times airplanes are not hijacked.

A terrorist is like an airplane crash. Sometimes airplanes crash and nobody knows when or where it will happen. We have a lot of people whose job it is to make flying airplanes safe. But even when an airplane crashes, we have to remember that there are thousands of airplanes that do not crash. The news on TV reports an airplane crash, but it doesn't report all the many times when planes are perfectly safe.

In the same way, we don't know when or where a terrorist might try to do something. But we are careful and have a lot of people working to protect us. If a terrorist does try to do something, it probably won't be near us, and there will be lots of places that are safe.

29 Do adults worry about the war too? What about the president? Does he worry?

Yes, they all worry about the war. That's why adults want to watch the news on TV so much when a war is going on. They are worried about our soldiers and want to know what is happening. A lot of adults have lived through other wars and know that it will hurt a lot of soldiers and their families. And they worry about that happening again.

A war is sort of like a bully on the playground. Sometimes we can avoid the bully and feel safe, but we worry about what the bully is doing. Other times we have to stand up to the bully and hope he will change. If we don't stand up to him, he may get worse.

Sometimes somebody fights the bully so that everyone can enjoy the playground again. If someone is going to fight the bully, many others are going to worry. They will worry about someone getting hurt. They will worry about what happens if the bully wins. So it is natural for us to worry when there is a war. Even the president worries.

30 Is it OK to cry?

Yes, it is. Crying does help you feel better, especially when you can cry with someone. Crying doesn't help us so much when we have to cry alone.

Crying helps because you are letting yourself feel what you are feeling instead of trying to hide your feelings. It isn't good for us always to try to hide our feelings. If you are sad, crying is a way to say to yourself and others, "I am sad." Crying helps you to release the churning you feel inside of you.

Sometimes when other people do not want you to cry, it is because crying makes them feel helpless. They think that if you are crying, they are supposed to fix your feelings. But when you are sad, or upset about a war, nobody can fix that. You just need to feel what you are feeling.

Other times, people don't want you to cry because then they will find out that they are sad also, and they don't want anyone else to know they are sad.

31 How does a soldier feel about being away from home?

Soldiers have different feelings about being away from home. Some of them have families that they really miss a lot. When they had to go to war, they had to leave their families behind. That is sad for them.

Many of our soldiers are very proud to be fighting for our country. They believe that they are fighting to preserve our freedom, so that our country can continue to be a good place to live.

Many of them are willing to talk about being afraid of what might happen to them when the fighting starts, but they look at what they do as being an important job — they have trained for it, and now they will do what they have to do.

A soldier's mother read her son's letter on a radio station. In his letter he said that he was following in the footsteps of many other American soldiers who in the past have fought for freedom. He also said that he was willing to give his life to help make the world a safer place for those he loved.

Not every soldier feels that way. Some joined the military and thought there would not be any wars. Sometimes a war happens and they have to fight. They may feel it is unfair, but no one can promise a soldier that he or she will not have to go to war. When a war does happen, even these people will do their job in order to protect their friends and those they love.

32 Why did war have to start while I am still alive?

That's a good question. Many of us wonder about things like that. No one knows what is going to happen in the future, so no one knows when a war will begin. Our leaders work very hard to keep war from happening, but sometimes a leader in another country comes along who wants war. So a war begins.

Almost every day of your life there has been a war going on someplace in the world. Most of the time it is a little war, so nobody knows much about it except those who live nearby. Those little wars do not affect us and do not even scare us.

Sometimes the war is big. Everyone knows about it, and it does scare us. Our leaders need to work hard to prevent wars, and we need to pray for peace.

33 How does the enemy feel?

Most of the time the enemy feels just like we do. The people in the enemy country are often afraid and do not want war. Even the enemy soldiers feel like our soldiers do. Sometimes they are afraid and do not want to die. Sometimes they want to surrender.

Many times, the enemy soldier is fighting because he is forced to by his country. Maybe he has been drafted by his country. Sometimes the enemy soldier is told that if he doesn't fight, the government will kill his family, so he fights to protect his family from his own country.

We sometimes forget that even the enemy soldier has a family. He has a mother and a father, sisters and brothers. He may have a wife and children of his own as well. So he may feel just like you do and wish the war would be over real soon.

34 Why am I afraid to die?

Everyone is afraid to die, even if we know Jesus. We want to enjoy our life here. When bad things happen in our world, we still want to live and enjoy life. Whenever we stop wanting to live, and want to die instead, we are really upset inside and need to talk to someone about what we are feeling.

Note to parents: Death is still one of the taboos of our culture. We do not like to talk about death, or even think about it, especially if we are talking about someone we love dying.

It is very difficult to explain to a child what death is all about. Children under the age of seven or eight do not even have the cognitive ability to understand what death is. Your child really does not need you to explain death, or even want you to talk about death. She is asking why she is afraid, and that is the part of the question you want to respond to. Whenever people die, and it touches your home through someone you know or through news broadcasts, children will experience these fears. It is important that they know these fears are normal, and that all of us feel them.

35 How do people feel when someone they love dies?

They feel very sad. We all feel sad when someone we like has to leave us. When someone dies, they leave us and they do not come back, so we feel very sad.

We may also feel angry that they left us. We will also feel angry at whatever it was that made them die. If they were sick and died, we may feel angry at sickness. We may be angry at the doctors for not making them better. If someone dies in war, we will be angry at the war. We will be angry at the leaders who made us go to war. We may even be angry at the person who died because they left us here without them. All of these feelings are OK to have, and everyone who loves that person will feel those feelings.

When someone dies in a war, we may also feel proud of them because they were willing to fight to protect us and make it safe for us back at home. We will still feel sad, but we can feel proud at the same time. It is not easy on us when someone we love dies. We may have a whole lot of different feelings at the same time, and that is why it is important to talk about what we are feeling — so we can clear up our confusion.

36 How can I be brave?

Sometimes we think brave people are those who do not cry. That is not true. Even brave people will cry. Brave people also will feel afraid. But if they are sad or if they are afraid, they know what they are feeling and are able to do what they have to do anyway.

All through our country's history, we have had many examples of people being brave. Sometimes they do dangerous things to help others find safety. Sometimes they do things they did not have to do, but they chose to do them because they felt it was the right thing.

Very few of us will ever have the opportunity to do something dangerous to show how brave we are. But we can still be brave. We can show how brave we are by doing the things that we are supposed to do, even when we don't feel like doing them. That may mean that you do your schoolwork, even when you don't feel like doing it. Or it may mean that you do extra things around the house to help out during the stressful times of war, even though it is not something you really want to do. That's being brave.

CHAPTER 3

Questions about the Enemy

37 Will terrorists attack our country?

Terrorists are people who attack innocent people at unexpected times and in unexpected places. They do this to get attention and to intimidate people. To intimidate means to bully someone and make them feel afraid. Terrorists bully people by doing terrible things to them.

During the war, you may have heard on the news that terrorists were sent out to our country to attack innocent people. Even now that the war is over, is this something you still worry about?

Well, we have people in our country whose job it is to protect us from terrorist attacks. There are people in the military, and there are special security people, and of course there are all the police too. All of them have all been trained to look for and stop terrorist attacks before they happen.

We also have specially trained dogs who can sniff out bombs before they have a chance to hurt anyone. The people who protect us also have all kinds of special equipment and machines made to help protect us against terrorists. So we really don't need to live in fear of terrorists. In fact, by not letting them scare us, they lose and we win.

Do you remember when the president made his State of the Union address? That's the big speech the president gives at the beginning of the year to all the leaders in our government. Someone suggested that he give the speech from inside the White House because of the possibility of terrorists. President Bush said that he refused to become a prisoner inside the White House because of fear, like the terrorists wanted him to do.

The president knows about all the people who work in this country to protect our freedom and safety. He was not afraid. He was confident that he would be safe. He went on with his work and his travels. We too can go about our daily lives and not have to worry about our country being attacked by terrorists.

This doesn't mean that we can be careless. We live in a world that has real dangers, including terrorists. As parents, we are here to teach you how to be aware of things which are dangerous so that you can be careful and stay safe.

38 Are our enemies bad people?

Our enemies are simply people on the other side in a fight or disagreement. Some people who are enemies in one fight can become friends in the next. It just depends on what the disagreement is all about, and which side of the disagreement we are on. Enemies are people just like us. They are both good and bad because they are people. No one is perfect or all good.

39 Should we pray for or against our enemies?

Well, that depends on what we are praying about. Sometimes prayer is a time to tell God all about how we are feeling — a time to get our feelings out.

In the Bible, King David prayed once when he was at war, only he prayed for God to break his enemies' teeth. That seems like an odd prayer. The Bible doesn't tell us how God answered David, but one thing we can learn from it, though, is that it is OK for us to talk to God about our feelings — even about the sad or angry feelings we have inside.

Kind David also prayed that God would stop the success of the evil things his enemies were doing. This is a good way to pray for the enemy, because we are told to hate what is evil. If we hate the evil things the enemy is doing, it makes sense for us to pray for the bad things to be stopped.

Jesus told us to love our enemies and to pray for those who hurt us. This is very hard to do. When we try this, though, something happens that is good for us, and probably good for our enemy too. When we pray for our enemies — for good things to happen to them — it helps us not to stay so angry and have so many uncomfortable feelings.

If there is a bully at your school, you might want to pray for him and ask God to bring good things into his life as well as take away the mean and bad things from him. Maybe the bully is a bully because nobody at his home really takes care of him or loves him very much. We can pray that God will bring more love into his life.

40 How can you love your enemy when they are hurting you?

The word *love* is sometimes used to describe a warm and wonderful feeling. Love can also describe the way we treat another person. Of course we are not going to have warm and wonderful feelings about someone who is hurting us. God doesn't expect us to let people hurt us or for us to smile while they hurt us. But we can be patient and kind. We can try not to let them make us jealous. We can make sure we don't brag in front of them. We can stop expecting to get our way all the time.

Sometimes the best way we can show love for our enemies is by standing up for what is right. It's not real love when we go along with something that isn't right or isn't fair. Love stands up for what is right. We can stand up for what we believe to be right, even though our enemy might disagree and be on a different side. We can even disagree with someone without hating them and treating them badly.

There is a story about a little boy who was stopped by three big bullies who were threatening to hurt him. There was no way he could fight and win. So he came up with an idea. He drew a line in the dirt and said, "I dare any of you to cross this line." One of the bigger boys stepped across the line with a mean look on his face.

The little boy smiled and said, "Good, now we're on the same side." Soon the other boy started to smile too, and then the other boys did also. When they were all smiling, there was no more tension. That's an example of turning an enemy into a friend by choosing to act with love.

41 Why do our enemies get mad at us and burn our flag?

The people who get mad at us usually see the world in a different way than we do. Anger can mean many things. Sometimes anger is a way of expressing how we feel when we don't think something is fair. Some people don't think it is fair that our country has so many nice things and uses up so much of the world's resources.

Sometimes anger is a way of expressing feelings of being stuck with a life that isn't happy. Some people may blame America for the things that they don't have. Sometimes anger can be a way of acting when we are afraid and we don't want anyone to know we are afraid. Maybe some of our enemies get mad at us because they are afraid of the power our country has.

One of the ways that our enemies can show us they are mad at us is to burn our flag. Every country honors its own flag. Our country does too, so when our enemies want us to know how angry they are, they sometimes burn our flag.

It is hard to understand where someone else's anger comes from. It is even harder to understand the anger of a large group of people. That is why it is so important that we keep talking with the people who think of us as an enemy. When we can understand each other better, maybe we won't be so angry and will find ways to work out our differences.

42 Why do we have so many enemies?

Often countries that are our enemies believe things about the world that are the opposite of what we believe. Our country believes in democracy and capitalism. That means that we believe that people have the right to choose their own leaders, the right to own land and property, and the right to run their own businesses if they want to. We believe that all people are created equal. We believe that if a person is allowed to learn and work hard, he will be able to become anything he wants to become. We believe in freedom for all of our people, even though we don't do everything perfectly to carry that out. We believe that it is the freedom people have in this country and the chance to get personal rewards for their own work that makes our country so rich and powerful.

Our nation is also a nation that recognizes God and puts our trust in God for our blessings. Our money says "In God We Trust." Our pledge of allegiance says "One nation under God, indivisible, with liberty and justice for all." We believe that God created people to be given freedom and to be protected; this makes the individual person very important. We do things to protect individual rights.

There is another way of looking at life that is very different from our point of view. It is called communism. The beliefs of communism are that no one should own property but that everything should be owned and controlled by the government. Communism says that everyone should work for the good of the whole group without working for themselves. It believes that the only way for communism to succeed is for everyone in the whole world to become communists.

Communism does not believe in individual freedoms. It does not let people freely choose their leaders, their jobs, or even where they can travel. It does not believe in liberty for its own people. Most of all, communism doesn't permit freedom of religion — the right to go to church.

We base our whole form of government on what is called the Judeo-Christian ethic. This means that we figured out our laws on the basis of what is taught in Jewish and Christian teachings. The communist nations base their government on the belief that there is no God. They require everyone in their government to be atheists, people who say there is no God. Instead of thinking that the individual person is important, communist nations say that the individual should serve the government. They do not believe that people were created special by God.

Remember, an enemy is someone who is on the other side of an argument. When our beliefs, values, and view of the world is different from the people of many different nations, it makes sense that we would be on different sides from them and that they might become our enemies.

43 Is the Soviet Union our enemy?

After the second big war in the world — World War II — the Soviet Union and America were on different sides in our views of how the world should be run. There was not a war going on between us and the Soviet Union. There was more of a contest to win the emotions and beliefs of people in smaller nations about how their countries should be run: either by communism or by democracy. This is what is called a cold war.

Now things seem to be changing in the world. People in countries that tried communism are admitting that it didn't work. Many countries that once believed in communism and didn't allow freedom are changing. Even the leaders of the Soviet Union are saying things that make many people believe the communists are changing their thinking about how the world should be run. They are allowing people in their country more freedom.

Since our two countries have grown to understand one another better and since their beliefs and actions are changing to agree more with our beliefs, the cold war is over. Freedom is spreading. This is what President Bush is talking about when he says that there is a "New World Order."

So, for the moment in the big picture of world events, the Soviets are not our enemy. But we need to remember that an enemy is someone who is on another side in a disagreement. There will be other disagreements that we will need to work through. In some of them it will not be surprising if the Soviet Union takes another side. A whole nation of people doesn't completely change its way of thinking about the world in just a few days.

44 If it's OK for countries to fight, is it OK for me to fight too?

The first thing to remember is that countries don't fight whenever they have a disagreement.

There are people paid by the governments of all countries whose only purpose is to try to talk things out and work out disagreements without the use of force. These people are called diplomats.

Fighting is the last choice for working out a disagreement between civilized countries. Most countries try to talk things out between themselves. Sometimes they turn to the leaders of stronger countries to help them. Some countries choose not to ever consider fighting as a way to deal with a problem. The countries who choose force as a way of dealing with their problems before trying everything else are not very well liked or accepted by the other nations of the world.

Whenever you have a disagreement with someone, there are many things you can do before you would have to think about fighting as a way of dealing with the problem. You can try to talk it out between yourselves and try to understand each other. You can call on someone stronger and older — someone such as your teacher or playground supervisor — to help you work it out. Think of a kid you know who deals with his problems by fighting without trying other ways first. He is probably not very well liked or accepted by the other kids. When you choose to fight as a way of handling problems, you will not have the kind of acceptance we all want.

Each family has values and rules to help you know when you might have no other choice but to fight. As strange as it sounds, fighting might be the only way to have peace, if you have tried all the other ways and none of them worked. Some of the reasons you may have to fight are: to defend yourself from danger, to defend someone who is defenseless, or to stop a bully who is hurting and scaring innocent people. Hopefully, all children will have a parent or caring adult whom they can turn to for protection. Children should not be left to defend themselves.

Parents want their kids to be safe and feel safe. There are different ways of helping you feel safe. There are some parents who don't believe that children should have to defend themselves and they want the child to feel safe by knowing that they will be protected without fighting. Other parents believe it is good for the child to feel confident by knowing how to defend themselves. This is something each family needs to talk about so that you can know what is expected of you.

45 How do the enemy and their families feel?

The enemy and their families are people just like you and your family. They are on the other side in a certain argument but they are not necessarily bad people. They may be fighting for something we feel is wrong but they may sincerely believe that what they are fighting for is right. They have all the same kinds of up and down feelings we have.

CHAPTER 4

Questions about God and War

46 Does God choose sides?

God is always on the side of what is right because it is God who made up the rules about what is right and what is wrong. He explains what is right in the Bible.

God doesn't change his mind about what is right and wrong. So, even though sometimes it looks like God chooses sides, it is really people who choose whether or not they will be on God's side.

If someone little is being hurt, or beat up by someone bigger, God is on the side of protecting the little person who can't defend himself. God wants people to be free, so when someone is taking away another person's freedom, God is on the side of protecting freedom.

Note to parents: The important point with this question is that we can choose to be on God's side by doing what's right. God is always on the side of right, and we can choose to be there with him.

47 Why are there so many wars in the Bible?

The Bible is a book about real people and their countries. Since God is telling us about these people, he tells us a lot of things about them, including the wars they fought. As long as there have been people, there have been misunderstandings, disagreements, fights, and wars.

The Bible was written so we could see how God is involved in the lives of people in all sorts of situations, including wars. Because we can see all sides of people, their good sides as well as their bad sides, it helps us learn right from wrong. It also helps us to know if we should fight in a war, and when a war is right.

48 Does God like war?

No, God does not like war. God loves everyone, no matter what side of the war they are on. And God doesn't like to see the people that he loves hurt each other.

The Bible tells us that one day God will make a new earth where there won't ever be any more wars. When God makes this new earth, there won't be war, or weapons, or pain, or crying — even the animals won't fight with each other! We will all live together in peace and harmony. But for now, we live in a world where things are not perfect. There are some things that God allows us to do, even though he doesn't like them.

49 Does God want freedom?

Freedom is one of the most important things to God. That's why God lets us choose even whether or not we will love him. God wants freedom for all people and all countries, but he gives us the freedom to decide if we want to enjoy his freedom or not.

When someone or some country has freedom and someone else tries to take it away from them, this is called oppression. The Bible tells us that God does not want people to be oppressed.

God wanted freedom so much that he sent Jesus to earth to help everyone find freedom from sin in their lives, even if they live in a country that does not have freedom.

50 Does God punish people who kill in a war?

God gave Moses the Ten Commandments, which shows all of us right from wrong and which helps us know what is right or wrong in our own lives. When we do things that are right or wrong, there are consequences to our deeds. What that means is that there are things that will happen based on how we act.

For example, if you do something your mom

or dad told you they wanted you to do, a result could be getting a reward. If your mom or dad told you never ever to do a certain thing, and you choose to do it anyway, a result might be that you would be punished. Can you think of a time when you obeyed and a good consequence happened? How about a time when you disobeyed and there was a bad consequence?

God has said to us, in one of the Ten Commandments, "You must not murder." Murder involves killing people, but it means the kind of killing that occurs when we are very angry and filled with hatred, or when for selfish reasons we want them dead.

The Bible talks about accidentally killing people. An accident is when we didn't mean for anything wrong or harmful to happen, but when something happens by mistake. God doesn't punish us for accidents. There are other times when God allowed killing in wars, or even told his servants to kill certain people, and it wasn't called murder. He didn't punish those people for what they did. They had obeyed him in going to war.

If someone you know is in the military and is fighting in a war, he is aiming at military targets and not at innocent people. He is not murdering people, like God talks about in the Ten Commandments. He is not killing someone for selfish reasons. Even if he accidentally killed someone who wasn't a soldier, God would not punish him.

God deals with us for what is in our hearts. He doesn't punish us for accidents. If we have to kill someone because it is our job in the military, and we are doing it to protect our freedom or to help someone else who is oppressed, God will not punish us for that.

51 Why does God let war happen?

God has let us have the freedom to choose whether we will do right or wrong. He has given everyone that freedom because it is so important to our lives. When people have freedom to choose, sometimes they make bad choices and that creates wars.

The Bible tells us that wars and fighting happen because of the way people are inside. When people have greed and selfishness in their heart, they start a fight in order to get what isn't theirs.

Many times when this happens, others who see this wrong being done will try to stop it by talking to the side that is doing the wrong thing. But sometimes talking isn't enough to make the bully stop doing bad things to other people. That's when sometimes it may be necessary to use force to stop a big bully from taking things that aren't his.

When countries do this, it is called war. God doesn't like war, but he lets it happen because he has given us freedom to choose for ourselves — even if our choice is to go to war.

52 Whom should we pray for?

We should be praying for everyone that we care about. God tells us we can bring all of our cares and worries to him because he cares for us. If we can give God all of our worries and anxieties, we don't have to be so afraid.

We should also pray for all the people who are our leaders. We can ask God to give them wisdom and courage, so that they will do the right thing.

We should also pray for the enemy and for their leaders and their families. We may not always feel like praying for our enemies, but God has asked us to pray for them, and it is good for us to do that. We can pray that they will be able to know what is right. We can also pray that God will protect the families and the children in countries where wars are being fought.

53 Does God love the enemy?

God loves everyone in the whole world. That means he loves the enemy, and even loves the enemy leaders who are making people die. Just because God loves the enemy, though, does not mean that he approves of the things they do when those things are wrong. God can still love the enemy and make sure that there are bad consequences for their bad behavior, and good consequences for their good behavior.

54 I'm mad at God about the war! Does that make God mad at me?

If you can say that you are mad at God about the war, that is really good, for it means that you know how you are feeling. God understands our feelings, and if we are mad at him, it doesn't upset him. All of us get mad at God sometimes.

You know how you sometimes get mad at Mom or Dad when you can't change things to be the way you want them? Do we still love you when you are mad at us? Of course we do. We love you even when you are angry at us, and God loves you even when you are angry at him.

Have you told God how you are feeling about him and what you wish he would do to help you feel better? Why don't you do that? Maybe it would help you and God to make up. God knows that this is very hard for us to do, and that is why he listens so carefully when we want to talk to him.

55 Does the Bible say when the world will end?

No, the Bible does not say when the world will end. Thinking about the end of the world can be very scary. What do you think of when you hear people talking about the world coming to an end?

Actually, the Bible does talk about the world coming to an end, but only so that we can have the beginning of a better world. It will be a new world where everyone is always safe, where there is no more war, no more sickness or death, and no more sadness or crying. It will be a beautiful new world where there is peace, and where people will always do what is right. In the new world, all people will love God and each other.

We don't know exactly when the old world will end. Some people think it may be soon because some of the signals that the Bible says will happen seem like some of the things happening now. What we can be sure of is that God tells us that we can hope for a new and better world to come. He also says that we should live like it could be at any time. But for each day, we are to live the best we can and love as much as we can and be at peace as much as we can in this world.

56 Is it wrong if I don't want the world to end?

Of course not. Most of us feel the same way. There are some really nice things about our world that all of us enjoy. Why don't you want the world to end?

Sometimes we can be afraid that too much is going to change and we might lose all the people who love us. You don't have to worry about that. We will take care of you; we aren't going to leave you alone. Neither is God. He promised that he would always love us and stay with us and take care of us, no matter what happens with this old world!

Note to parents: Depending on how your child answers the question in the first paragraph, your conversation could go in a number of different directions. Be sure that you address the real issue at the heart of their concern before you are tempted to talk about your perspective about the end of the world. What your child is probably concerned about is that she might be left alone when the end of the world comes.

CHAPTER 5

Questions about Peace and Peacemaking

57 Was Christ a pacifist?

There are many things Jesus said to help us understand that our Creator meant for us to live in peace with himself and with one another. He tells us that in his kingdom there is a way of doing things and a way of being together with God and with each other that is different from our world's way. It is a way of being together that happens when we are willing to love each other so much that we would rather be hurt ourselves than to hurt someone else. We would rather do what is best for another person even if they are wrong — even if they are our enemy. This is the way Christ Jesus loves us.

Jesus also tells us that this world still needs to be fixed, even though his love has begun to change some of the people in it. He is saying that we cannot expect to live in a perfect peace with one another until the world is fixed. War is never good, but sometimes it is necessary because the world is a place where bad people must be stopped from doing what is bad.

Jesus did not just sit back and allow people to

do whatever they wanted. When there were people in the temple more interested in money than God, he turned over their tables and chased them out of the temple. Christ conveyed to us in that bold move that sometimes we must take action and not just sit back and allow people to go on doing what is wrong.

58 How can you start a war and pray for peace at the same time?

Hitler was an evil man who killed many Jews before he killed himself. He killed himself because he was about to be captured by his enemy and punished for killing all of those Jews. If no one had fought him, he would not have stopped killing Jews. Few would say it would be wrong to fight an evil man like that. Most would pray while they did it.

In the Persian Gulf War, a country was stolen. The people of Kuwait, who had worked hard for their homes and property, had them stolen by the army of Saddam Hussein. We felt like they should be given back to those who owned them. If we did not stop Saddam Hussein from stealing people's things in one country he might have gone on to steal them in other countries. So we fought to stop him, to bring peace to the land,

and we drove Hussein out of Kuwait. And while we were fighting, we were praying all the time.

59 How can you be a Christian and fight in a war?

There are some Christians who think you cannot be a Christian and fight in a war. They are called pacifists. They believe that when Christ told us to turn the other cheek in our personal relationships, he meant for us to do that as a nation also. Most other Christians believe that although each person should try to be a peacemaker, when our country or another country is challenged by someone, we must fight to preserve freedom. That freedom allows us to be Christians or Muslims or Jews or whatever faith we want to be.

In many instances in our history there have been men who have hurt many thousands of people. Adolph Hitler was one of those people. We had to fight him to stop him from doing even more evil than he did. I believe there are times when God expects us to work with him against evil people who want to hurt others. There are many Christians who believe that by fighting for good, they are obeying God and serving him as Christians.

60 Why does someone surrender after fighting a war?

People surrender when they realize that they can no longer fight back and no longer do what they came to do. In a war, a military leader will usually surrender if he sees that the battle has been lost. He will surrender to keep his soldiers from being killed when there is nothing they can do to help. If a leader sees he is going to lose the war, he might surrender so he has a chance of staying in power. Sometimes, if the leaders in a country are very cruel, or are forcing soldiers to fight, their armies may be happy to surrender.

61 Can I do something to help keep peace between countries?

Something you can do any time of the day is pray. God hears people when they pray.

Prayer can seem confusing sometimes, especially if you think of people on two different sides in a war each praying for God to help them. But here is an example to think about: What if you and your friend walked to the park and found two children hitting each other or throwing things at each other. Maybe you would try to stop them by yelling at them. If they kept on hurting each other, you might try to find their parents so they could help stop the fighting. After you had done everything you could do, there would only be one thing left — ask God to help it be over as soon as possible.

Sometimes only God knows who is doing the right thing and who is doing the wrong thing in the war. Each person on both sides believes he is right. It can be very confusing. When we pray, we can pray that God will do what is right. We can pray that in all of the terrible fighting something good will come out of all of it.

There are some very simple things you can do that can be helpful during wartime and after. These things mean a lot to people you may not even know. Send letters to those in the military and thank them for the sacrifices they have made. Most likely you will get a letter back from someone who is very grateful that you wrote.

Sometimes people in the military have families back home that are in need of food and money. You can send them food and even collect money from you friends to give to them. You can write letters to those families and tell them you are praying for them and the family members that are away during war.

There are a lot of leaders that care a lot about what little people think and feel. You can send a drawing or a short letter to a world leader in hopes of helping him think about what he or she is doing. It is a great thing to want to help. Just because you are young does not mean that you cannot help.

Look in the back of this book for other ideas about activities you can do.

62 Is the "peace in your heart" that you read about in the Bible the same as peace after a war?

No, they are not the same. Peace after a war means that no fighting is going on. It does not refer to how people feel. It's possible for people to not be fighting but still feel a lot of anger or fear. Now that the Persian Gulf War is over, we might say there is peace, but many people — especially the people of Kuwait and Iraq — have great fear and sadness and anger in their hearts.

Peace in your heart, according to the Bible, happens when you trust God and no longer are afraid or angry. A person who has peace in her heart is a happy person, satisfied that she is living the right way and doing the right things. In a world where there are many problems, it is wonderful to be able to have peace in your heart. If you do not, you will worry about everything. You will not be a very happy person.

CHAPTER 6

Questions about Patriotism and Politics

63 **Why do we put up flags during a war?**
You probably already know that each star on the
flag of the United States stands for one of the fifty
states. The stars on the flag seem to say that just
as the stars look as though they are always there
in the sky together, the states will stay together too.

When people fly flags, I think that what the
people are trying to say is that they, too, want to
stay together with all the other people of our
country, just like the stars in the sky and the
states in our country. Most of them are saying
that they believe the war must be fought, even
though they may want very much not to have to
fight it. They "support" the war, and especially
the men and women who have offered their lives
to help the country fight a war. But some of
them are saying that they will support our
country and the people who must fight in the
war, even though they do not believe that
deciding to fight a war is the right way to solve
problems with another country. They are all
reminding each other that, even though the
country is going through a hard time, they have

decided to stay connected with one another. And they are reminding the people who are fighting the war that their mothers, fathers, brothers, sisters, and friends (and even strangers) appreciate the very hard things they must do. People fly the American flag to show their support for the country.

64 Why are some flags only halfway up a pole?

In our country, we have a custom — a certain thing that we have done over and over again through many years. It is a way for us to tell everyone that someone we care about has offered to serve his or her country, and that person has died while serving. It is our custom to lower the flags we fly to "half mast" (to halfway down the pole) when someone we love has died in service to our country. We do this because we miss that person very much, and because we want others to know what that person has done and how much they meant to us. After all, there may not be many people who will ever know that person's name. From now on, when you see a flag flying at half mast, you will know that a family has lost someone very important in the war. And if you see all the flags flying that way, you will know that someone very important to many people in the country has died.

65 Why did some people protest the war?

Some people protest war because they know how much wars hurt people, animals, the earth we live on, and other things that mean a lot to us. They do not believe that war helps to solve problems between nations, and they don't believe that war does anything good at all. Many of these people believe that when groups of people disagree with one another, or when one group hurts another group, the best thing to do is to try to talk to one another and solve the problem without fighting. They believe that if we try hard enough and long enough to understand what other people feel and think and need, and if we are "fair" and willing to change ourselves, then war will not be necessary at all. When something is bad, like another country wanting to fight us, the protesters believe we should try to overcome them with good instead of more bad like war. They would say that if someone else has done something wrong, it will not help for us to do wrong also.

If a friend hits you and you hit back, it starts a fight. If a friend hits you and you forgive the person, there is a chance that you will build a relationship rather than destroy each other. That's a good way to act with the people around us, but it doesn't always work so well between countries.

Other people protest war because they believe God does not want them to fight a war, no matter what the reason. Some of these people, like the Quakers and the Mennonites, are groups of Christians. They remember that Jesus Christ said some things once, while he was teaching a large group of his followers on a hillside in Palestine, about how his kingdom is different from the kingdoms, or nations, of this world. He said we should love our neighbors in the same way we love ourselves, the same way we want to be loved. Some Christians believe that Jesus taught that in every case it is wrong to fight back and it is our duty to love other people the same way God loved us.

Also there are people of different religious faiths who protest war because they believe war is always wrong. A very famous man from India named Ghandi worked all his life for peace in his country. He and all the other people who don't believe war is ever OK are called pacifists because they believe we should live in peace with each other no matter what.

Pacifists usually believe that it is OK to resist something they think is wrong by drawing attention to their cause. They may do this by not eating or by lying down in people's way and not moving. These are the kinds of protests you see on TV. This is called "passive resistance." Gandhi resisted the fighting among different groups of people in India by saying that he would not eat any more food until the fighting stopped and the people agreed to live peacefully with one another.

So far we have told you about people who protest war because they believe that war is always wrong, but there are many people who protest some wars and not others, who think that there are times when war is necessary and right, and sometimes it is not. These people sometimes believe that their country is fighting a war for wrong reasons like just to make itself richer or to make someone believe something different about God. So people who might not have wanted us to fight in Vietnam would probably see the need for us to fight Hitler when he killed many Jews just because he did not like them.

In the Persian Gulf War, some people protested because they thought we just wanted to get richer off all of the oil over there. Others saw our need to fight to prevent other leaders from stealing another country.

People protest war because they do not like war, and they want it to end as soon as possible.

66 Why are coffins covered with flags?

When someone dies in battle or while serving our country in other important ways, it is our custom to cover that person's coffin with the American flag. This is to honor them, to show the other people of our country that they have paid the highest price possible in order to serve our country. To honor these heroes in this way is a way of showing their families how thankful we are for the sacrifice made by the person who was killed or died.

67 Could the president make a mistake and get us into war needlessly?

No one does everything right every time they try to do something. Our world is often a very difficult place to live in. No one except Jesus is perfect. Since the president is not perfect, he could make a mistake.

To prevent that from happening, the president has many smart people working for him. When a very tough decision has to be made, he asks for all the people that work with him to help him make the best decision. This does not prevent all mistakes from being made, but it helps avoid many of them.

Another thing that helps the president is that there are certain things that the president cannot do without approval. He has to ask people in Congress if he can do certain things. Going to war is one of those things he usually cannot do on his own. He has to have approval from the Congress.

We elect the president because we think he can do a good job. Sometimes we think he is making a mistake because we do not know everything about a very tough problem. The most helpful thing we can do is pray for our president, asking God to help the president make very few mistakes and that if he does make a mistake, it will only be a small one.

68 What is Veterans Day?

Veterans Day is a holiday we celebrate on November 11 each year. It is when our country takes time to remember two terrible wars, World War I and World War II. For years we have honored those who fought in those wars. People who were in the military and actually fought in a battle are called veterans. More recently Veterans Day has been used to honor those who fought and served in other wars such as the Korean and the Vietnam War. In the future, Veterans Day will be a time to honor those who served in the Persian Gulf War as well. Veteran's Day is a wonderful time to find an older person who has fought in a war and ask that person to tell you stories about the war and what they did to help the country. You should also thank that person for serving our country so you can live in freedom.

69 Why do we have holidays that celebrate wars?

It does look like we have some holidays that celebrate the terrible tragedy of war. Fourth of July and Veterans Day are two days that are like that.

But there is another way to explain why we celebrate these holidays. What most people are glad about is not war. They are really saying how happy they are that the war is over. And they are glad if they believe that something wrong has been made right. Men and women who have been willing to serve their country in a war are part of the celebration too. When we celebrate the end of a war, or the beginning of what we believe it has accomplished, we tell those who served in the war that we are grateful to them for doing what they have had to do. We tell them that their friends who have died in the war are remembered and appreciated. But this does not mean that anyone wants to fight another war. It means that we will all remember together what the war cost us and what we believe it may have accomplished.

70 What does it mean to be patriotic?

A patriotic person is someone who loves our country and shows it. A patriotic man or woman might cry when "The Star Spangled Banner" is played. Patriotic people feel proud when they see a flag blowing in the wind. They are loyal to our country and support it in many ways. They might fly their own flag, do volunteer work to help the community, or even fight in a war. All of these are ways to be patriotic.

It seems that patriotic people have a special love for their country. They appreciate the freedoms we have here. And the red, white, and blue flag seems to have a special meaning for them. It represents how wonderful it is to be part of this great country.

71 What if I don't feel like cheering for my country?

During a war, most of us want very much to feel like cheering for our country. We want to believe that our country is doing what is right and we want to show our support. There will always be times for most of us when we don't feel like cheering for our country, or our friends, or our mom and dad. No matter how much we want to be able to cheer for them, we just don't feel like it. Because we have different feelings at different times, there will come a time when you will be sad and not very cheerful.

Sometimes we do not feel like cheering because we feel like we are losing. Sometimes you might not feel like cheering because you don't know what is happening. The best thing you can do when you feel confused or sad is to talk about those feelings. Asking me questions and telling me about how you feel may make the bad feelings go away.

If you think about it, you can probably figure out why you do not feel cheerful. Are you sad because you hear about so many people getting hurt or dying and you can't understand why things have to be that way? Are you afraid that your country is doing something wrong by fighting this war? Are you upset with what other people are saying about the war or about the country? Do you cry sometimes, and think that our world seems all mixed up about right things and wrong things? Do you get angry because you can't understand, or do you think there is nothing you can do? Feelings like this are not bad or wrong, but what you do with them is very important.

72 Why do some people not like our country?

Some people have been raised in a different country and they do not understand how great it is to live in a country where you can live in freedom. Others living in this country do not agree with all of the things our country does. They might not like it because they believe we have not been fair with some people like the American Indians who were here before anyone else. They might not like us because they do not think we do enough for poor people or old people. These are just some of the reasons they might not like our country.

There are many people in other countries who do not like our country because they are jealous of all of the things we enjoy in America. You know how this feels if you have a friend who has a better bicycle or toy than you do. If you don't talk to someone about those feelings, you might come to dislike your friend just because they have something you want. That is why some people do not like us.

With billions of people in the world, no one will ever agree on everything. It is not surprising that while many people love this country, there are some people who do not.

CHAPTER 7

Questions about What Happens After a War Is Over

73 How can we know when a war is over?

We can know that a war is over when there is a written peace treaty between the nations or groups that went to war. A treaty is a written agreement that the war is over. In a treaty, everything is explained clearly so countries later on can't change what they promised to do.

Treaties have to be signed by someone who has the authority to represent the whole government of a country. This person could be a president, a prime minister, a king, or some other leader.

When both sides have come to an agreement, written it down, made it open for everyone to see, and have it signed by people who have the power to speak for their country, the war is considered to be over and both sides are expected to keep their promises made in the treaty.

The other way to know a war is over is when one side is beaten so badly that they give up and go home. They may still be angry and not sign a treaty, but they have lost so many soldiers and machines that they can't fight anymore.

74 How does a war end?

A war comes to an end when one or both sides are convinced to stop fighting. Some of the things that happen near the end of a war are advance, retreat, withdrawal, cease-fire, armistice, and surrender.

An *advance* is when one side moves forward with their military forces to try to push back the enemy or cut their forces off from their supplies. The goal of an advance is to get the enemy to run away or give up the fight or to take away a place that is important to the military leaders.

A *withdrawal* is when one side moves back. Sometimes troops will withdraw so that they can plan a new way to go to reach their goals.

A *cease-fire* is when both sides agree to take a time out from the fighting, but they have not come to an agreement about what they were fighting about.

An *armistice* is a written agreement to stop fighting for a while.

A *surrender* is when one side decides to give up fighting and put down its weapons. A surrender needs to be given in writing, by someone in authority and delivered to the leaders of the other side. A surrender can't be just a rumor of something someone says because it could just be a way to trick the other side.

75 What happens after a war is over?

After a war is over, many things happen for the countries involved. Wars are fought because someone is trying to change something. When the war is over, those changes are made. These are sometimes called peaceful changes.

After a war, all the countries go back to talking and decide the new way things are going to be. The side that won the war gets to decide things, while the side that lost the war doesn't get very many choices.

After a war the things that were destroyed need to be rebuilt. In the talks after the war, all the nations involved, and sometimes the United Nations, decide who is going to help pay for the rebuilding. This payment is called *reparations*. This was one of the questions that delayed the ending of the Persian Gulf War. First, the enemy did not want to pay for anything. Then gradually, it agreed with the United Nations resolutions that said it had to pay.

Another thing that happens after a war is that the countries decide what will need to be done to make sure no one starts the fighting again. Sometimes there is a group of soldiers from many different nations that represent the United Nations, who stay in the area as a peacekeeping force.

Sometimes it takes force to keep the peace. It's kind of like when you know that your parents or teachers have the power to discipline you and this helps you choose to obey. A peacekeeping force can keep some countries from breaking the peace treaty. Usually the side that won the war keeps some of their soldiers there for that reason.

Another thing that can happen after a war is war trials. These trials are held to hold the leaders who did not follow the rules responsible for their actions and to punish them for the bad things they did.

After a war, people try to learn lessons from the war so that we can keep from having more wars in the future.

76 What will happen to my family after the war?

If someone in our family was hurt in the war, or even died in the war, we would need to make some changes in order to rebuild our lives and deal with the feelings we have.

When something bad happens in our lives, or in our family, it is natural to feel deep feelings of sadness and hurt. The process of working through our feelings after something bad happens is called grief, or grieving.

If you have to grieve about something that happened to your family in the war, you will feel some of these feelings:

You will first deny that something bad happened. You will have feelings like, "I just can't believe this happened!" or "I don't even want to hear about it."

You will feel angry at what happened. You will be angry at those that made it happen. You will be angry at our leaders for not protecting you and your family. You may even be angry at God for not stopping it from happening.

You will try to make bargains in your mind to make it seem as if what happened didn't really happen. You may think things like, "Maybe if I behave better, then this won't be true," or "God, if I become a minister, then maybe you will change what happened," or some other thought that tries to make a deal with God or someone else in order to change things.

You will also feel very, very sad. It is called depression. This kind of depression is where you get very angry at yourself and say things like, "I should have behaved better," or "I should have prayed more" or," Why didn't I just stop them from going to the war?" When you are in this stage, you blame yourself a lot for the bad thing that happened to your family.

Acceptance is the final stage. This is where you are still sad, but you know that the bad thing really happened and that no one, not even God, can do anything to make things different.

When you are feeling any of these feelings, it is important that you talk with someone you trust and love. Even if that person feels the same way, it helps when you talk about it together. One thing to remember is that you will get through these feelings and life will be happy again. But it is important that you go through the whole grieving process.

77 Why can't all of the soldiers come home right after a war is over?

We need to remember it is the job of our armed forces to work to keep our country safe. When a war is first over there are still a lot of strong feelings and unsettled emotions. There is the danger that the war could start up again, just like there is the danger a fire can start easily when the hot coals are still red. To make sure that the war doesn't start again, some of our soldiers will be needed to stay in the area for a while to help discourage anyone who would want to start trouble.

78 When will our soldiers come home?

Soldiers are under the command of their leaders.
They go off to the war to fight and stay there
until everything is done. When that job is done,
they may be sent to another place where they are
needed. Most of the soldiers come home just a
few weeks after a war is over. Before they leave,
the leaders must think that the war will not start
up again in that same area.

79 Will we let the prisoners of war go free?

When a war is over, everyone is supposed to let
the prisoners that they captured go free. It is part
of the Geneva Convention, the meeting where
everyone decided how wars should be fought.
We let the prisoners go just like we are supposed
to. We work out the time and place with
everyone and insure that they are returned safely.

Often when we capture a prisoner, we treat
him better than his own country treated him. In
the Persian Gulf War, some of the prisoners we
captured didn't want to go back to their own
country because they were afraid of how they'd
be treated back home. Often we give prisoners
more food and water than they were getting. We

want prisoners to know that we are a good country by treating them well.

80 When will my nightmares stop?

A nightmare is a very bad dream that scares us. No one knows exactly why we have nightmares, but they are a sign that something has scared us badly. Usually the nightmares go away when we are not afraid anymore. You can talk to a grown-up you trust and tell him about the things you are afraid of. Sometimes we are afraid of things that really can't hurt us. If you can talk about what you're afraid of or draw pictures of it, maybe we can help you put away some of your fears.

Sometimes nightmares are our mind's way of trying to understand something that is very confusing and scary. Keep talking to us about what you don't understand. There are also groups of other children who are upset by the war who meet together to talk to each other about what they are thinking and feeling. You could find out about one of these groups through your school or the nearest military base in their family services office.

Note to parents: You may wish to contact one of the resources listed in the back of the book for professional counsel for your child.

81 Why can't I stop thinking about the war?

Our minds are amazing. We are created with a desire to know and understand the things that affect our lives. The war has touched all of our lives, and it's normal to want to understand. Once our mind thinks of a question, we will keep wondering about it until we understand. This is sometimes called curiosity. Curiosity is very good because it encourages us to learn. You are learning and getting answers for your questions from this book. Once you understand the answers to the things you're curious about, you probably won't think about the war very much more.

If we ignore our curiosity and don't find answers for our questions about the war, or hide our questions because we think they are dumb questions, we may still be bothered with thinking about war for a long time. Remember, there are no dumb questions about war.

82 Will there be another war?

No one likes war. War is one of the worst things that can happen anytime. World leaders throughout history have tried to make a world that does not have wars. For now, we live in a world where war is something real that we have to deal with, even though no one likes it.

The Bible predicts a day when there will be no more war, when the world will be at peace. The New Testament says that this day will come when Jesus Christ, the Prince of Peace, comes back to earth to make everything right that has been wrong.

The Old Testament talks of a coming day when peace will rule, when we won't need weapons to defend ourselves anymore, and no one will even need to learn about war (Isa. 2:4-5).

We can all hope for the day when there will be no more war. Even now when we live in a world where wars sometimes happen, the Bible tells us to seek peace and to look for the peaceful way out of disagreements whenever possible.

So for now, when a war is over, we can be thankful that it is over. We can hope and pray for a world where there will be perfect peace, and we can try as hard as we can to be at peace with everyone we know.

83 How does someone surrender?

One of the ways that a soldier can surrender is to carry a white flag, or something that looks like a white flag. This is a recognized symbol of surrender. When someone raises his hands above his head and is not carrying a weapon, this also is a sign of surrender.

When countries want to surrender, they will often tell someone who is acting as a peacemaker that they want to surrender. In the Persian Gulf War, the enemy communicated to the United Nations their intentions. They brought a letter that was delivered by their ambassador.

84 What do soldiers do after a war?

They will do different things. Some of them are in what is called the reserves. These are people who have been in the military, are trained, and then were discharged from active duty in the military. They returned home and found jobs working in what is called the civilian part of our country. They would go to monthly reserve meetings to continue their training and also go on training duty for several weeks in the summer.

When the reservists come home from a war, they are sent back home to their civilian jobs. We have people in the reserves to do just that — to be a backup to our regular troops. Most of them will stay in the reserves, just in case they are needed again in the future.

The people who are in the military as a full-time job will come home to their military base, and go back to work doing what they were doing before the war. They will also continue to train so that they will be ready in case they are needed to help somewhere in the world.

85 Why am I still mad even though the war is over?

We may still be mad, or even sad or worried, after the war is over for several reasons. For one thing, we are often mad after a war because we find out some more of the bad things that the enemy soldiers did to innocent people. This new information will keep us feeling mad.

Another reason we are still mad may be because we are still upset by the bad things that happened in the war. People that we know, or that are related to people that we know, were hurt or killed by what happened in the war. One of the things we will feel is sadness, or grieving. A big part of sadness, or grieving, is being angry at the bad things that have happened, and to be angry at the people who did the bad things.

Another reason we may still be mad is that it takes a long time for all the parts of a war to be settled. After a war is over, countries take a long time arguing about who is going to pay for the damage, how much it is going to cost, what soldiers will stay in the area, and other things like that. When we hear about these things on the television, it reminds us of the bad things that happened during the war, and the bad feelings that we had.

CHAPTER 8

Questions from Children Who Have Parents in the Military

86 Why does Dad have to go and fight?

Editor's note: For the sake of clarity and simplicity, some of the questions in this chapter refer to the father as the parent who serves in the military. This is not meant to diminish the role of women in the United States military or overlook the situation where a mother is the parent who serves. Furthermore, it is not intended to ignore the possibility that both parents might be in military service. The masculine nouns and pronouns are used here to keep the wording of answers as simple as possible for young children. The editor encourages the parent, grandparents, relatives, or friends who are caring for children of a parent in military service to adapt these answers to the situation at hand.

Sometimes parents have to leave home to protect other people in our country or in another country. Just as a policeman leaves his family to protect those who live in your neighborhood, a soldier does the same thing in another part of the world.

Moms and dads in the military train and work hard to be the best protectors they can be. No one wants to send them off to fight in a war. But if they did not go, some bully from another country might want to take our country away from us. A bully might start by taking over a small country. Our country wants to protect the world from mean people like that. Your dad is doing a wonderful thing for our country and for the whole world with his willingness to fight in a war.

Other people in our country who do not go and fight because they have not been trained are very thankful that your dad is willing to do this hard job. They also know that it is not easy for you to say good-bye to one of your parents. In a real way your sacrifice and your sharing your parent with the world makes you one of the heroes of war. There are many people across this country and around the world that are praying for you as you miss your dad. They are also praying that your dad will come home to you safely very soon.

87 Why did he leave me behind? I wanted to go with him.

You wanted to go because you love your dad. Your dad did not want to leave you behind. He is missing you very much. He loves you even though he had to go and fight, knowing that you would be left behind.

One of the reasons he left you behind is because he does love you so much. Where he is going it is very dangerous. He has worked and trained hard to know how to live in a dangerous place. While you were playing or working in school, he was getting ready to be brave and win the war. Since you have not been trained, it would be dangerous for you to go. The chances that you might be killed or hurt are much greater than for your parents, who are prepared to fight the enemy.

Your dad is your boss. He tells you what you have to do and you do it. Sometimes you don't want to do it but you do it anyway. The leaders of our country are the bosses of your dad when he goes to work. They have told your dad where to show up to fight the war. They have asked him to leave you here. Although he does not want to leave you, he has to because the boss said so.

88 Did I do something wrong to make my dad go away?

No, there is nothing you could do that would make your dad go away. He loves you no matter what you do. He asks you to be good, but even if you were very bad he would still love you a lot. He loves you, and every minute he is away from you he wishes he were with you. Rather than you being the reason he left, you are the reason he would like to leave where he is and return home to you. If the country did not need him so badly, he would do that right now.

Please believe me when I say that this is not your fault. I know that some children feel guilty if their parents leave. They think if they had been better boys or girls they would not have gone away. Sometimes they think God is being mean to them because of something bad they did. If you ever feel this way, just tell me about it. If you need to ask me every day if this is your fault, I will be happy to repeat every day that it is *not* your fault and you do not need to feel badly because of being away from your dad.

89 Why is it hard for me to sleep?

I don't know for sure why you can't sleep. It could be because of some of the scary things on television about the war. It could be that you are imagining scary things about the war. Some children get scary pictures in their minds when they close their eyes. Have you ever had that happen to you? I have too. Can you tell me about what the pictures are like?

You know, you can change the pictures. When you think of a scary thing, you can tell yourself to think of a fun thing like Disneyland or swimming or eating a chocolate birthday cake. The next time you have a scary picture, try to put a nice picture in its place. Then let's talk about that scary picture and the nice one both.

Some children feel afraid to be alone at night. When someone we love is far away, it's normal to feel afraid or maybe angry or sad or guilty. Those feelings don't feel too good, do they? Well, they can feel even worse when we are alone or very quiet. Could that be why you are having trouble sleeping? Me too.

90 What will my dad be doing when he goes off to war?

Your dad has have a very important job that is needed to help keep our country safe. As long as he continues to work hard at protecting our country, you can grow up and be anything you want to be. That is what freedom is all about, getting to choose what you want to do.

When he is away, he gets up early in the morning, gets dressed, washes his face, brushes his teeth, and does all of the other things you do in the morning. He eats breakfast, lunch, and dinner. The food is not as good as it is at home, but it can be quite good. There are other moms and dads who are away from their families too. Some of them are there to make sure your dad has enough food to eat and a warm place to sleep. This helps your dad stay strong and healthy so he can do his job well.

Every night when your dad goes to bed he has a quiet time. That is when he takes time to read letters you write and look at pictures you draw. It is the best part of his day—when he thinks of you and looks at things you send him. Imagine your dad lying on a narrow bed on top of a green blanket holding a picture of you or reading a letter you wrote. Imagine a big smile on a face that loves you very much. That's what moms and dads do when they go off to fight a war.

91 I miss Dad. What can I do?

Let's send him a note, or we could draw a picture, or maybe go to the store and buy some of his favorite cookies and send those over.

I will be your secretary. You tell me all the things you want to say, and I will write them down. Then we will send it, so he knows exactly what you are thinking about. Anytime dad gets a letter or a picture from you, it is very special. Sometimes it takes a long time for our mail to get to them, but the more we send the more he gets, and that helps him feel close to us.

There is something you can do that does not take as long as letters and pictures. You can pray. I know he would be thankful if every day, or every time you thought of it, you would pray for him and his safe return.

92 Will Dad get shot or will a missile land on his head?

Getting shot is one of the dangerous things about war. There are lots of people in the military with your dad, and they are all working very hard to protect each other while they protect our country. Most of the people who go away to do their job in a war will come back home to their families when they are finished doing their job. What's really sad is that some of them might get shot. But very few get shot. Most of them come home safely without ever being hurt.

Do you really worry about this a lot? Sometimes I do too. You know what helps me? It helps me to think about all the great things they have to protect them. Let's think about that. What are some of the things you can think of? There are helmets, and big airplanes, and missiles that shoot down other missiles. There are also thousands of people who are working together every minute to protect your dad from all of the dangers.

93 Who can I talk to when I need to talk?

Well, I'm here and I love you very much. I want to hear anything you have to say. You can talk to me about anything you think about and I will even keep it a secret if you didn't want me to tell anyone else. Did you know that there are counselors at your school who care about you and understand how you feel? Well, there are and you can talk to them anytime you need to talk. Or we could go to one of the school counselors together and both talk if you want to. There are other people who love you and would love to talk to you.

Note to parent or caretaker: Provide the child with the names of friends, grandparents, Sunday school teachers, pastors, and others you trust who have a loving relationship with your child.

There are plenty of people who care about you and want to listen to what you have to say. The worst thing you could do is be afraid or wonder about something and not talk to anyone about it. The best thing you can do is talk things out.

There are many other people around us who are going through the same things we are. Sometimes it really is good to know that we're not alone and that other people know how we feel. Did you know that there are other kids who would like to be your friend and would listen to what you want to talk about? They get together to be friends and to listen to each other and care about each other. We could let you get to know them and then you could talk to them too. Do you think you might like that? We could try it and see how you feel.

94 Will my dad get captured by the enemy?

Almost all of the people who are in a war will not get captured. So, this is something we usually don't have to worry about. Do you think you know what would happen if your dad gets caught? Is this something you think about a lot? If he was captured, he could still come home after the war is over. Have you ever played a game where if you get caught by the other team you have to stay out of the game until it's over? Like maybe dodge ball or freeze tag? Well when someone gets caught in a war, he has to be out of it until the war is over. Then when the war is over, the rules say that both sides let the ones who were captured go back home to their families. Sometimes, like in freeze tag, someone from their side can come in and rescue them. If that happens, then they either come home or they might go back and help do their job again. We don't know.

Note to parents: How much you should tell your child about details of life in POW camps depends on their age, degree of inquisitiveness, and maturity level. There is no reason to fill their thoughts with fearful possibilities of things that could be happening. There is great value in shielding them from ideas and images that will spark fears they do not already have. Even though it is possible that some POWs will die in captivity, we don't need to bring this up if they are not worried about it. If they bring it up, then deal with the issue of death in an appropriate way.

95 Does God know how bad I feel?

God does know how bad you feel. God loves you
very much and when you feel bad, it makes him sad
too. You know what? God sees every tear you cry,
even when you're alone. The Bible says that he
even saves them in a bottle up in heaven (Ps. 56:8).
That is what brave King David said God does
when we cry. Did you know that even brave kings
cry sometimes? God knows that sometimes life
can hurt really bad, and then we feel really bad
and God knows. Someday God will make a world
where we won't feel bad anymore and people
won't fight wars anymore. But for now, in this
world, he knows that we all feel bad sometimes. Do
you know what he did to help us when we feel
bad? He gave us each other so we could love each
other the way he loves us. And I'm here so that
when you're feeling bad I can tell you how much
I love you, and I can hold you and hug you and
love you while you're feeling that way. That is
one reason God let me be here with you.

There is something else I want you to remember
when you feel real bad. You won't always feel
bad. In fact, you will be happy again too. And there
will be some days when you'll almost forget
how bad you're feeling right now. I love you.

CHAPTER 9

Questions Parents Ask

96 How much war coverage should my children see on TV?

The answer depends on the age of your child, emotional makeup, and how he responds to what he has seen. Older children, ages ten to twelve, have a much greater ability to understand and tolerate what they see on television than do younger children. They can watch about the same amount of war coverage as you can, though they may quit before you do and go do something else.

It is advisable to limit the amount of time younger children spend watching the war on television. You need to monitor their reactions and watch for symptoms identified in the beginning chapter of the book. The younger the child, the more likely she will respond more to the visual images and sounds than to the words of commentators. Even the music used by television stations can have an effect on a younger child.

Whatever the child watches on TV should be discussed and put into a framework that integrates with her understanding of the world. It is more important that these discussions focus on how the child feels about what she has seen than on the facts surrounding what has been viewed.

During and after the Persian Gulf War, television coverage became a part of our daily lives. As parents, during wartime we need to be careful how much war coverage we allow into our homes. We may want to take some steps to isolate our viewing of the news to times or places that shield our children and protect them from being overloaded by images and sounds of war. On the other hand, we don't want to isolate our children from what is happening, for they will hear about it from their friends. It is better they hear about it in your presence so you can be aware of their reactions.

Keep in mind that after a war is over TV networks can still display some horrifying things on the TV screen. In fact, sometimes it is in the aftermath of war, as cameras are allowed onto the battlefield, that casualties are more vividly depicted and atrocities are discovered. This has been the case following the Persian Gulf War, as Americans have seen the horrors inflicted upon the people of Kuwait during Iraqi occupation. Just because the war has ended, don't assume the sounds and images of war on TV have ended as well. Continue to monitor your children's viewing.

97 How can I help my young child understand what is happening?

Children under the age of five will be most affected by how the war is affecting those around them. If Mom or Dad is upset, the young child will be dramatically affected since he perceives the emotional world through the eyes of those he loves.

What a child needs to understand is that he is loved, that he is safe, and that he will be protected. He needs to be hugged, held, and reassured frequently. He needs to be reminded often that Mom and Dad will make certain that he will be taken care of. If you are not in the military, make it clear that you will not be leaving him to go off to war.

98 How can I help my school-age children to understand what is happening?

Although school-age children may have a list of specific questions, their basic need still is to understand that they are safe. They know that war is scary and that it is having an effect on the people around them. As parents, we can help them by giving them more physical affection, hugging them and holding them to help them feel secure.

It is also important that we keep as normal a routine as possible in their lives. It may be helpful to take extra time before bed to talk, read, or pray together — little things that will help them feel close to you.

At this age, children are able to articulate their fears, feelings, and questions. We need to be sensitive to them, listening carefully to find out what they understand and what conclusions they are drawing. They need to be free to express whatever is going on inside of them, their emotions and thoughts, without being shamed. Sometimes it helps them express themselves if they draw pictures of what they are feeling. Playing war games also helps them to act out some of their feelings.

Once we have a complete picture of what they are experiencing, we will be better able to help them process their feelings and understand the family's values and feelings about war. It is important to validate what they are sharing with you. Say things like, "It's OK to feel what you are feeling," or, "There are no wrong feelings, so don't feel silly talking about what's inside."

Parents often feel they know what their child is feeling, and so they stop listening. This is especially true when a child has difficulty expressing herself. It is important that we be patient as we listen, encouraging her to continue talking with us.

Children ages five to nine still have a limited understanding of distance and the size of the earth. A globe can be very helpful in showing them how far we are from the war. In terms of the Persian Gulf War, use a piece of string to measure how far it is between Baghdad and Saudi Arabia, and between Baghdad and Israel. Then let the child try to make that piece of string reach where you live. This will show him how safe he is from missiles landing on your house.

Children ages ten to twelve are mentally capable of understanding the concepts of war, patriotism, duty, heroism, pacifism, and death. This newly developing understanding can pose problems of its own. For instance, a child this age may have strong feelings about killing being wrong. Yet he feels like cheering for our side to win the war. If he has a parent serving in the war, he may believe that he should be supporting our troops, but he is still angry at his parent for leaving.

This split between the emotional self and the intellectual self can be terribly confusing to children. We can help children this age by encouraging them to talk about their thoughts and feelings and to take them seriously when they do. Then we can help them sort through their emerging beliefs instead of halting the process by telling them what they "should" think or feel.

99 Should children be allowed to see dead soldiers on television?

No. There is no positive effect to having children view wounded or dead soldiers on television. In the Persian Gulf War, this became more a problem after the war had ended. Reporters were allowed onto the battlefield; we saw more images of the wounded and dead on TV than we had during the previous forty days of aerial bombing. Childhood is a time when children need to be shielded from some of the realities of life until they can be understood.

In dealing with death in a family setting, we can use traditions, religious beliefs, and the ceremony of a funeral or memorial service to help us deal with the passage from life into death. Even when presented in its best light, death is mysterious and quite frightening. War is death at its worst, without any boundaries to protect the child's inquisitive mind.

100 Should I just turn off the television until the war is over?

Each parent needs to make this decision on the basis of his own family and children. However, shutting off the television will not keep the war out of our children's lives.

War is one of the painful realities of life. Turning off the television will not insulate our children from those realities, but it may slow down the pace at which our kids are exposed to these events. If we choose to turn off the television, we can use newspapers and magazines to help expose our children to war in a more controlled fashion. The printed media is easier for us to control and makes less of an impact on our children than television.

To ignore the war completely is unrealistic. Children will be exposed to the war through their peers and school. Pretending that the war is not happening also causes us to miss out on an important opportunity to help our children develop skills for dealing with life and for developing values.

Instead of turning off the television completely, we can use the crisis of war to help our children learn to control what they take into their minds. We can also help them understand the principle of moderation.

101 What if I am having trouble caring for my children because I am glued to the television?

If our children begin to act out aggressively or show other signs that they are being overwhelmed by the war, it may be because we are watching too much war coverage on the television and neglecting them in the process. One of the key issues raised for children by the war is their fear of abandonment. If we are obsessed with watching the war on television to the point that we are emotionally absent from our children, they will experience feelings of abandonment.

If we are so emotionally upset by war that we are having problems functioning in day-to-day life, we need to get some help for ourselves. The best thing we can do for our kids is to take care of our own emotional needs and to be supported by other caring adults in our life. This helps prepare us to take care of our children's emotional needs.

If we don't take care of our own emotional needs, our children will key into our own pain and anxiety and either mirror what we feel or act like they are responsible for taking care of us. Either of these patterns can be harmful to our families.

Although it is only natural that our children can be a source of comfort to us in times of crisis, it is important that we not rely on them as our primary source of emotional support. We need to be their primary source of emotional support. If this is difficult for us, we need to find our emotional support from other adults in our life. This needs to be a priority for any parent.

102 My spouse is away from our family fighting in the war. How can I deal with my own emotions and still take care of my child?

With one parent away from the home because of the war, with no guarantee of their safe return, your child will already be experiencing feelings of abandonment. If you are so emotionally drained that you are emotionally absent from your child, then your child is experiencing abandonment from you as well. It is important that you get help for this as quickly as possible.

Often events like war cause old feelings of unresolved abandonment from our own childhood to come to the surface in our own lives. Whatever the cause of your own emotional distress, there are support groups available to help you. Check with the family services office on your local military base, or contact one of the resources listed at the back of this book.

Your feelings are just as important and just as valid as your child's feelings. However, you are

in a position to find help for your emotional
needs, whereas your child is not in that position.
Since your family is already missing one
important member, your child cannot afford for
you to be overwhelmed by your needs and be
unavailable to him.

103 Is it bad for kids to play war games?

Sometimes yes and sometimes no. It all depends
on your child and the way you respond to their
play. Whether we like it or not, children play
war games. We probably all have played war
games sometime when we were kids. Children
have been playing war games in most civilizations
in most cultures throughout history. It is unrealistic
to think that playing a war game will stop
because we declare a ban on them.

War games can help children work out some
of their anxiety about war. They get to act out
some of their fears and in doing so can have a
clearer picture of what they are feeling. If your
children play war games, talk to them about
their game. Ask them what rules they have and
how they know who wins and who loses. Again,
this gives you opportunity to talk with them and
better understand how they are responding to the
war news they are hearing.

In many cultures, playing war games is an important part of peer association and male bonding. War games don't have to be preparation for physical violence. In a sense, life can be seen as a series of battles where we need to develop the characteristics of a good soldier. Even the Apostle Paul used the illustration of being a good soldier in his New Testament letter to young Timothy.

With some direction, pretending to be a good soldier can teach children several things. They can learn how to cooperate with a team. They can learn how to build a human support system and develop discipline, self-denial, and physical stamina. Values such as loyalty, perseverance, patience, and protecting people who are too weak to protect themselves can be experienced. Other values that war play can help develop include courage, determination, endurance, security, planning, and sacrifice.

If the man who is the role model for his son happens to be a soldier, playing soldier can be a healthy part of the bonding process between father and son. In this case, playing war games may be a means of working out feelings about the absent soldier father as well as helping to maintain a strong bond with the father while he is away.

104 Should we buy war toys for our kids?

It seems to be a part of the human experience for
most children, especially boys, to display an
interest in war toys. This is true even when the
parents may hold strong pacifistic convictions
and find war toys to be offensive.

This interest within children can be very
frustrating to the parent. Even if parents will not
buy war toys, kids are very resourceful at creating
their own. Tinkertoys make excellent weapons.
Even without Tinkertoys, a tree branch can be a
rifle or missile launcher. So is it realistic to expect
our children to conform to our values?

The key is finding balance and responding to
your child's interests and curiosity about war.
Remember, to a child, war games are games.
Playing with war toys can give children a sense of
power and control that will help them deal with
their own fears.

If you see your child playing with war toys, or
creating his own war toys, try to talk to him about
what he is doing. Use this as an opportunity to
guide and direct him as he plays. Show him ways
he can play with these toys that will help him
express to you some of his feelings and fears.

If the parent forces a toy gun into the hands of
an uninterested child, or if the parent forbids a

child to play with war toys and delivers a severe lecture when he finds his child playing with war toys — either approach runs the risk of helping create within the child an obsession with war and the tools of war.

Following the Persian Gulf War, it seems likely that Americans both young and old, will embrace a new generation of heroes. Your child's war play may be a way of identifying with the young men and women in the military who are now coming back to the States. This emulation of heroes is healthy and should be encouraged.

105 Is watching the war on television different from watching a war movie in terms of its effect on children?

Yes, there is definitely a difference. Kids are well attuned to their parents reactions and will react to whatever emotional climate is created within their family. Adults have different emotional reactions to watching a real war on television versus watching a movie about war.

The immediacy of today's communication systems calls for real human compassion. If we are watching someone on camera while an air raid siren wails and we see that person duck for cover, there is tension over the potential of what might be happening right before our eyes. When we watch Isaac Stern playing a violin concert with everyone in the audience wearing a gas mask, we are confronted by the life and death issues of war. If we hear that a SCUD missile has landed on one of our troop barracks, we are moved with concern and compassion. When our children watch these news reports with us, they feel not only what we are feeling, but their own feelings of fear and anxiety as well. They know there is a difference between these events and a war movie.

If your child knows someone whose parent or parents are fighting in the war, this will add to her fears and concerns. The thought that something could fall arbitrarily from the sky, killing and maiming innocent people, makes anyone who understands ponder the fearful possibilities for their own lives. Children have imaginations that are largely unfettered by experience. Viewing war as it unfolds can suggest many terrifying jumping off points for the imagination. Unlike the movies, there is no way to tell ourselves that it is only a story.

106 How can I help my child not feel so powerless and afraid during a time of crisis?

In the Chinese language, the idea of crisis is conveyed with two characters of their alphabet. One means danger and the other means opportunity. When we are in crisis, our kids will be aware of the sense of danger. We need to help them see the opportunity they have to learn better how to deal with life and with challenges and change.

Long after the war is over they can be stronger people because of the lessons they have learned, which have shown them that they are not powerless when bad things happen in their lives.

One of the reasons children may become more aggressive or even regressive in their behavior during a time of crisis is that they feel powerless. The crisis affects their family life and their world in proportions that feel overwhelming. We need to find ways to give back to them some sense of control and power in the situation. Here are some suggestions:

Help them find ways to express their feelings. You can encourage them to draw pictures of the war and anything that they are worried about. Let them talk about their feelings, and never shame them or embarrass them for expressing honest emotions.

If they are old enough, you can let them write about their feelings. If they need to cry or otherwise express emotions that they do not have words for, comfort them as they try to put their feelings into words. Don't tell them to stuff their feelings by saying things like, "Big boys don't cry," or "Don't cry. Daddy wouldn't want you to be crying."

Help them use role-playing games to work out their own solutions to their fears. For example, there was one mother who noticed that her four-year-old son was being more aggressive than usual in his play. Instead of just scolding him for the aggression, she began to play with him, trying to find out what was going on inside of him. She asked, "What are you fighting?"

"A giant scary dragon," he answered.

"What does he look like?" she asked.

In response, he described a very frightening spectacle.

"Oh. Are you afraid?" the mother said.

The little boy nodded yes.

"Well," mother asked, "what could you do to protect yourself?"

The boy worked his way through a number of options for dealing with the imaginary yet scary monster. He said he could get Dad to chase it away. But since his dad wouldn't be home for a while, he could run away and hide. Then he decided he could run into the back yard and climb up on the roof.

"Can the dragon fly up on the roof, too?" Mom asked.

"Yes," the boy answered, "but I will climb into the little window on the roof, and the dragon is too big to get in that window, so he will just have to go away."

That was the end of that particular fear and the little boy's unusually aggressive behavior.

When we let our kids use supervised play or fantasy to process their fears, they can think things through until they are convinced they are safe. Even though their fears may be imagined or based on something they have seen and perhaps misinterpreted, their fears are real to them.

We can help them resolve these fears and gain a sense of power by working their fears out in play. This also gives us a wonderful opportunity to get to know what they are thinking and feeling so that we can comfort them appropriately.

Help them feel significant. Our kids need to feel like they can do something to help. Let them call the White House comment line and give their opinion. The number is (202) 456-1111. Get the name of your state representative or senator and help them express their opinions in a letter. Think of ways they can do things for the soldiers or their families. Consult the activity ideas and resources at the back of this book for further help.

If a parent, or both parents, are involved in the military, children need to maintain as normal a life as possible. They will find security in the familiar and predictable family routines. You can reinforce this by celebrating birthdays and holidays in creative ways. Take pictures and send them to the absent parent as a means of staying in touch.

Be a good role model of learning to cope in healthy ways. We need to do things that let us overcome our own feelings of powerlessness and develop coping skills for ourselves. When they see us coping, they will imitate us and be better able to overcome their fears and their feelings of helplessness.

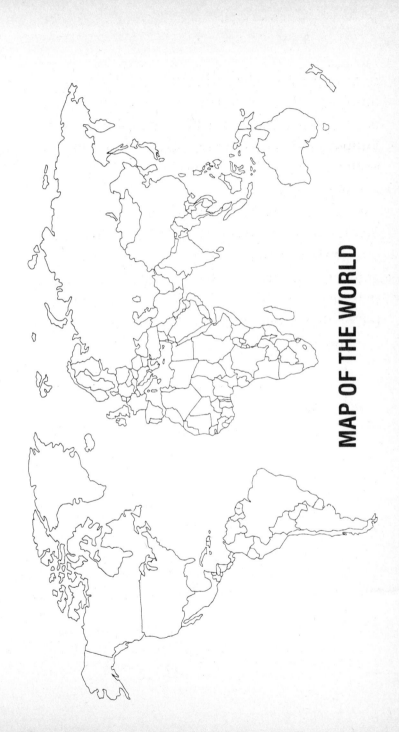

MAP OF THE WORLD

CHAPTER 10

Questions about the Persian Gulf War

107 Where is the Persian Gulf?

The Persian Gulf is a place far away from us on the other side of the world. When it is daytime here, it is night there. If you look at the map on page 159 of this book, you can see that it is right above Africa, which is also a long, long way away from us. The war took place in the countries of Saudi Arabia, Kuwait, Iraq, and Israel.

108 Can Iraq's bombs reach our country?

Note to parents: Provide a short piece of string the length of the distance between Iraq and Israel. Hold one end of this string on the edge of Iraq. Their missiles can only go as far as this string reaches on the map.

It is impossible for bombs from Iraq to reach us. Look again at the map. Do you see where Iraq is? OK, take a piece of string. Now look at where we live on the map. Pretend the string is on the end of a missile. Is there any way it can reach us? No! See, we don't have to worry about that. But if you do get worried, you can tell me and I'll try to help you feel better.

109 Do we have a right to be in the Persian Gulf?

If men with weapons broke into a home in this country and killed anyone who stood in their way, then stole what they wanted and said the house was now theirs, wouldn't it be right to stop them? That is what happened to the people of Kuwait. The leaders of Kuwait asked our country to help them get their homes back and make the people who stole their land go away.

The people in the country next to Kuwait, the Saudi Arabians, were afraid that the army from Iraq would also come into their country and steal their houses and kill their people. So they also asked the United States, and other countries, to come to their country to help protect them.

If someone is doing wrong to someone else, and won't stop when they are told to, most of us believe that it is all right to force them to stop. It is all right to make people obey the rules and laws that keep us all safe. That's what were doing in the Persian Gulf.

110 How did the war start?

There was an argument between the leader of Iraq and the leaders of Kuwait. Some of it was about oil, and some of it was about money. The leader of Iraq wanted to tell the people of Kuwait how to run their country. The people of Kuwait would not do what Saddam Hussein demanded, so the army of Iraq invaded the much smaller country of Kuwait.

Many of the people of Kuwait had nice homes and nice things. The army of Iraq stole whatever they saw that they liked. They arrested thousands of Kuwaiti people and put them into jail without a trial. All over that little country, they hurt people very badly, even killing innocent people who were not in the military. Then they said that the country belonged to them now, and that they would never leave or give it back to the people who owned it.

It is against the laws of the world to do these things. No country is allowed just to come into another country and take whatever they want just because they are strong and can overpower the other country.

There is an organization called the United Nations that gets together people from most of the countries in the world. They met and told the Iraqi leader to stop and give the country back to the rightful owners. Many people from many countries tried to talk to him to get him to listen. They took away some of his privileges, and wouldn't let anybody sell anything to the Iraqis, hoping that would change his mind and his behavior. Still he wouldn't obey.

Then he captured innocent people, even children, from many different countries who were visiting Iraq and Kuwait. He wouldn't let them go home to their families. He forced them stay in Iraq when they wanted to go home instead. He even put them in dangerous places in front of his army to try to protect himself.

After the countries in the United Nations had tried everything they could, they realized that Saddam Hussein wasn't going to listen or do what they asked him to do. They tried talking to him for 166 days. Then they decided, as a last resort, that they had to make him obey in order to protect the other people in that area. That's when twenty-nine countries agreed to work together to make the army of Iraq get out of Kuwait. And that's when the war started.

111 Didn't anyone tell Saddam Hussein that he was wrong? Why didn't someone tell his mother?

Many people from many different countries tried to tell Saddam Hussein that he was wrong: other Arab leaders, leaders from countries that were friendly toward Iraq, and leaders that Iraq didn't really trust.

The United Nations Security Council, which is made up of people representing countries all over the world, agreed on what needed to be said to Saddam Hussein, and tried to tell him that he was wrong. They wrote it down very clearly and gave it to him in writing. The twelve parts of what they wrote are called United Nations Security Council resolutions.

Our government tried to talk things out in every way they knew how. One of our leaders, Secretary of State James Baker, went on ten trips all over the world and had more than 200 meetings talking to world leaders and trying to figure out how to get Iraq to listen and obey the law.

Even the top person in the United Nations, the Secretary General Perez de Cuellar, went to Saddam Hussein to tell him to stop, but the Iraqi leader refused to listen. Saddam Hussein didn't listen to anyone. I don't think he would have even listened to his mother, do you?

It was only after everyone involved had talked things over in every way they could think of, and nothing worked, that they decided that they had to force Saddam Hussein to do what was right.

112 Are we there because of oil?

Yes, partly. Oil is very important to the whole world. Oil gives us energy to keep many things that people need running and working. Because people need oil to make so many things go, oil is worth a lot of money. And when people control the production of oil, they make a lot of money and they have a lot of power. So if someone bad could get control of a lot of the world's oil, he would have a lot of power to do bad things in the world.

There are many oil wells in Kuwait and in the other countries in the Middle East. Just before the Persian Gulf War, Iraq used a lot of their oil and their money to fight a war against Iran. Saddam Hussein wanted more oil, more money from that oil, and more power. He was in an argument about all of this with Kuwait, and he didn't like the way the argument was turning out, so he started a fight.

Have you ever seen a bully do something like that? Well, he was acting like a big bully. He didn't get his way so he started a fight because he was bigger. He probably didn't expect anyone to try and stop him.

Saddam Hussein tried to steal all of Kuwait's oil, and even started to try to get the oil that is in Saudi Arabia. If he had been able to get all that oil, he would have been one of the most powerful people in the world.

Because he has shown that he is a very mean man and does not respect the laws of the world, it would be dangerous to everyone in the whole world if he had that much power. The other nations of the world agreed that we had to stop someone like that from getting all that oil and the power it would give him. They believed they needed to stop him to keep the world safe for everyone.

113 Why don't we just leave them alone?

When you are at recess, is there someone who is on the playground to make certain that everyone is following the rules and playing safely? If you were playing at recess and minding the rules of your game, and someone much bigger came into the game you were playing and broke all the rules, what would you say?

What if you told them that they weren't playing fair, and they said, "So . . . ?" and started to beat you up? Then what if they got some of their big friends to come and beat up your friends and take away your toys. Would you want the person on playground duty to just leave you alone, or would you want them to come and make big kids stop?

The Persian Gulf War was a lot like that. Kuwait is like the little kids on the playground. Saddam Hussein and the Iraqi army are like the bully and his big friends. The United Nations and the twenty-nine nations trying to help Kuwait are the person on playground duty, whose job is to protect everyone. If we hadn't done something to stop the behavior of Saddam Hussein and his army, the world would end up not being safe for anyone, and the bullies would take over.

114 What places and people did we bomb?

We aimed our bombs at what are called military targets. We didn't fire our bombs just anywhere in Iraq or Kuwait because we didn't want to hurt the people of those countries. We just wanted to stop the army of Iraq and get them out of Kuwait.

We aimed our bombs at the things which allowed Saddam Hussein to kill people, to shoot down our airplanes, and to talk to his army. Military targets are things like their weapons, ships, tanks, and places they store ammunition.

We also targeted the places that helped the Iraqis talk to the army out in the battlefield — places like radio and television stations, telephone wires and cables, satellite dishes, and radio towers. Another target for our bombs were areas that allowed them to travel with their weapons, like airports, roads, bridges, and railroad tracks. These are the places we bombed.

115 Were we bombing innocent people who weren't in the army?

Our bombs are built with computers and television cameras in them so they are very smart and go right to the military targets that we want to hit. We developed these kinds of bombs so that we could avoid hitting innocent people. Our soldiers didn't aim weapons at people who weren't in the armed forces; but they didn't always hit the target perfectly.

They did hit the targets most of the time. Sometimes, if innocent people Were close to a military target, they may have been hit. Sometimes we believed a target was a military target, but there were innocent people inside, and they got hurt. Our soldiers were trying very hard, and even took great risks with their own lives, in order to hit military targets and not hurt innocent people.

Some reasons that it might seem like we bombed innocent people is that Saddam Hussein let television cameras show damage only to areas that he says are not military targets. One time he even bombed a building himself and said we did it. Iraq wouldn't let us take pictures of the military targets we bombed, so it might have seemed like we were just bombing innocent people. We weren't.

In the Persian Gulf War, the Iraqi army put many of their military installations near civilian areas so that it would keep us from bombing them. They did this because they knew that our military people did not want to hurt innocent people. They also disguised some of their military places to look like other kinds of buildings so that it would confuse us. I'm sure that sometimes we got confused, but our intention was never to bomb innocent people.

116 Did Saddam Hussein use chemical weapons?

Chemical warfare is where germs or chemical gases are released into the air in order to try to kill people. Chemical warfare is against the laws of the world because it kills anyone who breathes in the gases, not just the people who are fighting in the army. The law says that people who aren't in the fighting are not supposed to be targets in a war, so no one is supposed to use chemical weapons.

Saddam Hussein has broken this law before. He used chemical weapons twice: once in a war with the neighboring country of Iran, and once against a group of his own people, the Kurds. Saddam Hussein has ignored the law in the past and bragged that he would use chemical weapons whenever he wants to. He threatened to use chemical weapons against Israel (a country that was not even in the war) and against the countries that were involved in the war.

One of the first things our airplanes tried to do in the Persian Gulf War was to destroy all of the places Saddam Hussein had hidden chemical weapons and the places where he made them. Chemical weapons were not used in the Persian Gulf War, and maybe it was because our pilots destroyed many of Iraq's chemical weapons before they could use them.

117 Are there children in Iraq?

Yes, there are children in Iraq. Iraq is a country with more than 12 million people. It has about as many people as the state of Pennsylvania. They live in a area about the size of California. The 12 million people in Iraq include families with mothers and fathers and children. One of the reasons so many people tried to work out the problem without having a war is because children everywhere should be protected.

There are children in Kuwait, too. Some of them were hurt and killed by the Iraqi army. When a leader of a country decides that they don't have to go by the rules, the world becomes less safe for everyone, even children. It is very sad and scary when children are not safe. Do you feel sad or scared about this? I feel sad. But I am here to protect you.

118 Why don't we just kill Saddam Hussein?

It is against the rules of war to target the leader of the country for death. That is called assassination. It is allowed in a war for the leader to be killed if he is hit inside a military target.

Saddam Hussein made himself very hard to find during the Persian Gulf War. He was hiding so that no one could kill him. He has spent lots of money to buy almost every kind of protection known to us today. He hid in a room that was reported to be sixty feet underground. That's like going down six floors into the ground. The walls and the ceiling are very thick to protect him from bombs. He also had a lot of bodyguards around him.

In the past, he has killed anyone he thought might even be thinking about assassinating him, even if they were relatives. There have been some of his own Iraqi people who have tried to assassinate him so that they could have a new leader. When their plan was discovered, they were killed immediately.

119 Why is Saddam Hussein so stupid and crazy?

We don't know that Saddam Hussein is either stupid or crazy. Some people think he is just selfish and cruel and greedy. Sometimes people can be smart and sane and still do terrible things. Saddam Hussein has been able to become one of the most powerful men in the world. He probably could not do that if he were really crazy or stupid.

What makes Saddam Hussein do things that seem crazy or stupid is something called *lawlessness*. Lawlessness is worse than just breaking a law. It means that you think you can ignore all the laws and do whatever you want. When a person is lawless he is very dangerous because he has no respect for the rights of other people. He has no respect for anything, except what he wants.

Saddam Hussein has shown lawlessness in many ways. He has killed whole groups of people just because he didn't like them. No one stopped him. Then he decided that he wanted to take over Kuwait and make it part of Iraq. So he ignored all the laws and just sent his armed forces in to take it for him. He told his army to steal and kill and destroy. He started shooting

SCUD missiles at innocent people instead of fighting against military targets. He decided to dump millions of gallons of oil into the gulf, showing no respect for the animals, fish, or birds. He set the oil on fire in the gulf and in Kuwait, which caused other problems for our environment. It showed that he has no respect for the other people who have to breathe the air.

When the armed forces of the other nations stood up to him and started to take back Kuwait, he set more oil wells on fire, burning up 17 million dollars' worth of oil a day. He did this because he did not want anyone else to have the oil if he couldn't have it.

All of these things make us think that he is crazy or stupid. It's hard for people who respect the lives of other people and respect the law to understand how someone could do these things. All of these things make more sense to us if we realize that he is showing lawlessness.

When Hussein wasn't stopped for the things he did before that were against the law, he thought he could get away with more. This time twenty-nine nations of the world stopped him. They showed everyone that this is still a world where there is right and wrong, and where people still have to obey the law.

120 Was this war predicted in the Bible?

In some of the books in the Bible, God told people about things that would happen in the future. He did this so that when these things happened, they would know that God is in control. It can help us feel safe to realize that God knows everything even before it happens and that he isn't scared by it.

Sometimes the Bible can be hard to understand, and different people have different ideas about exactly what God is trying to say. So don't feel bad if you're a little confused about what the Bible says about events today.

Note to parents: For younger children, it may be confusing and frightening to discuss Bible prophecy since their cognitive abilities are not able to understand or deal with the concept of God's foreknowledge of events, much less the controversy and speculation that surrounds many discussion of Bible prophecy. Younger children will probably not ask this question. If they do, it is probably because they heard someone else discussing it. It is best simply to reassure them that God knows what is happening, and that they will be safe.

With older children, there seems to be a fascination with anything supernatural and prophetic. This curiosity can be an open door to help them explore new ideas, discuss your family values, and direct them toward an interest in the Bible. If you do not feel comfortable discussing this with them, you may want to have a church youth pastor or one of your church leaders come over and discuss this subject with your whole family. You may want to read or discuss the following with children who are older than eight or nine.

There are some parts of the Bible which tell about things that seem to be happening today related to the Persian Gulf War. In the book of Jeremiah, chapters 50 and 51, there are prophecies that talk about the nation of ancient Babylon. What was once Babylon is now Iraq. The ruins of the ancient city of Babylon are about 60 miles from Baghdad and are partially rebuilt as a tourist attraction.

Some of the things foretold by Jeremiah happened just like God said they would — when Babylon was taken over by the Medes and the Persians a long time ago. Another part of these chapters talks about a group of many nations coming together to fight and win against Babylon. It also talks about Babylon attacking Israel, which has also happened many times in the past.

Some people believe that this describes what has happened in Operation Desert Storm. In Jeremiah 51:2, it talks about God raising up "a destroying wind" against Babylon. The Hebrew word which was translated as "a destroying wind" is the word *ruwaoh*. This is a word that can accurately be used to describe the desert storms which happen in that area.

Some people think that this could have been a play on words that God used so that we would believe that he already knew what was going to happen in Operation Desert Storm, and then believe in him more.

121 Is Saddam Hussein the Antichrist?

Whenever there has been a fight that involved many nations, people have wondered if one of the leaders would be what the Bible calls the Antichrist. Many people thought that Hitler was the Antichrist during World War II because he was so evil and caused so much destruction.

There are two key things that make it seem very unlikely that Saddam Hussein will be the final evil world leader the Bible calls the Antichrist. For one thing, most people who study the Bible's predictions for the future and who believe that there will be a real person as the Antichrist do not believe that he will come from Iraq.

The other reason is the Antichrist will bring peace to the Middle East by signing a peace treaty with the nation of Israel before the world realizes that he is evil. There is very little doubt in anyone's mind that Saddam Hussein would ever bring peace to the Middle East, or that he would ever make peace with Israel.

122 Why can't we just tell Saddam Hussein about God?

Saddam Hussein says that he already believes in God. He even says that he believes that God wanted him to do the things he is did. Since he already has his own strong beliefs, he probably would not listen to someone telling him about God.

123 What is an Arab?

An Arab is a member of a certain race or nationality of people who come from the Middle East. Their ancestors are all related to each other, so they have many things in common with each other. Do you know what nationality you are?

Your nationality has more to do with your ancestors and where they came from than just what nation you live in now. In America there are many different races or nationalities of people. Can you think of any of them?

Arabs now live in many different countries. If most of the people living in a country are Arabs, and all of their ancestors were Arabs, than that country is called an Arab country. Most Arabs live in Arab countries in the area of the Middle East, but there are Arab people who live in many different places around the world, including our country.

Iraq is an Arab country. So are Kuwait and Saudi Arabia. There were also several other Arab countries who fought against Iraq. There are a few Arab countries that are friends with Iraq. And then there were some Arab countries who simply refused to fight at all.

Just like any other race or nationality, the Arabs will be alike in many ways. This is because people of the same race share the same background, traditions, and history. Many people of the same race hold beliefs that are alike also. But people who are the same race are still individual people who can think for themselves and be themselves. So we cannot judge all Arab people by what someone like Saddam Hussein is like.

When we judge someone before we get to know him, just because we may have known another person of the same nationality, that isn't fair. This is called prejudice, or racism. Can you think of how prejudice or racism can hurt people? We need to be very careful not to dislike Arab people just because we don't like Saddam Hussein and we know he is an Arab.

124 Are the Arabs our enemies?

An enemy is someone we are fighting against. In this war, Saddam Hussein and his army were our enemies. Saddam and his army are Arabs, so some Arabs are our enemies. There are also Arabs who have been on our side in the Persian Gulf War. We have fought alongside the Arab people from Saudi Arabia, Kuwait, Egypt, Syria, and other countries. There are even Arab American soldiers in our military. So, no, all Arabs are not our enemies, but in the Persian Gulf War some Arabs were our enemies.

125 Do Arabs in Iraq believe in God, like us?

Most Arabs are Moslems, which means that their religion is Islam. There are a small number of Arab people in Iraq who are Christians — about 4 percent. There are even a fewer number who are Iraqi Jews. The Iraqi Jews are descendants from the Jews who were taken to Babylon as slaves a long time ago.

The Moslem Arabs believe in Allah as God. The Christian Arabs believe in Jesus Christ and the God of the Bible as their God. The Jews believe in the God of the Old Testament as their God. All three groups believe that there is only one God who is the creator of heaven and earth.

126 What is Islam?

Islam is the second largest religion in the world. The people who believe in the Islamic religion are called Moslems. Most Moslems live in the part of the world called the Middle East. There are two main groups in Islam: the Sunnis and Shiites. Ninety percent of the Moslems are Sunni Moslems.

The book of Islam is called the Koran. The Moslem believes that the Koran was revealed by God to the prophet Mohammed through the Archangel Gabriel. It is a book of laws and military and social codes. The Moslem believes that the Koran contains only the word of God and nothing human.

While Islam respects some of the people told about in the Bible, such as Adam, Abraham, Moses, Solomon, and Jesus, they believe that the final and best messenger of God was the prophet Mohammed. Jesus Christ is not accepted as the Son of God. If fact, a Moslem is horrified at the idea that Jesus is the same as God. "There is only one God, and his name is Allah," they say. They also do not believe that people need someone else to pay for their sins.

There are five things a Moslem does to practice his religion:

1. Saying the creed, which is "God is great. There is no God but Allah, and Mohammed is his prophet."
2. Praying daily, at five appointed times throughout the day, bowing toward the holy city of Mecca, which is in Saudi Arabia.

3. Fasting, especially during the month of
   Ramadan. When they fast, they fast from
   sunup to sundown. When the sun is down
   they can eat.
4. Giving alms, which means they give money
   or help to people who are poor and in need.
5. Going on a pilgrimage, at least once in their
   life, to the holy city of Mecca.

Another central belief in Islam is that God
hates injustice and oppression. Moslems believe
that God requires kindness to orphans and poor
people. They also oppose the drinking of alcohol
and the eating of pork.

127 How do the Iraqi people feel?

Iraqi people are people just like us. They love
their families. They worry about the war. They
care deeply about their loved ones who are in
the war. They feel all the same kinds of
emotions that we feel — love, sadness, pride,
fear, hope, grief, happiness, joy, anger, surprise,
worry, and guilt.

One thing about feelings is that they are just as
real and strong about something that isn't true,
but which we believe is true, as they are about
something that really is true. When someone can
control the things we know and believe, they
can control many of our feelings too.

It's like this: What if a robber came up to you with his hand in a bag and his finger pointing to look like a gun? If he poked you and said he had a gun, you would be just as afraid whether he had a real gun or were just pretending he had a gun by using his finger. In that situation, you are told that something is true that isn't true, and you are just as afraid as if it were true.

In Iraq, the people do not have the freedom to know the truth the way we do. The only information they are given is what Saddam Hussein wants them to believe. The government there controls what they see on television, what they hear on the radio, and what they read in magazines and newspapers. Sometimes the information they are given is false.

For example, when our ground forces first went into Kuwait and Iraq, we saw pictures on the television showing many Iraqi soldiers surrendering, and not very many of them even fighting. The Iraqi people were told lies. They were told that their soldiers were fighting and winning. They were not told that any of their soldiers were giving up.

In this case, the Iraqi people probably felt very happy and excited that their soldiers are winning even when it isn't true. Later on many have felt confused and angry that they were tricked into believing a lie.

128 Who fought on our side against Iraq?

There were twenty-nine nations that fought in the
war, and there was a total of thirty-three nations
that actively supported Operation Desert Storm.
Here is a list of those countries: Argentina,
Australia, Bahrain, Bangladesh, Belgium, Canada,
China, Chad, Denmark, Egypt, France, Germany,
Great Britain, Greece, Hungary, Italy, Japan, Kuwait,
Morocco, the Netherlands, New Zealand, Niger,
Norway, Oman, Poland, Qatar, Saudi Arabia,
Senegal, South Korea, Spain, Syria, United Arab
Emirates, and the United States of America.

All of these countries supported the war effort
in some way, such as giving money, medical
help, or diplomatic help.

129 Does Saddam Hussein have a family?

Yes. In 1963, Saddam Hussein married his first
cousin, Sajida Hhairallah Talfah. She is a
primary school teacher in Iraq. He has two sons
and two daughters. He is devoted to his family.
Before the war started, he sent his family away
from Iraq, so they would be safe from the
danger of being in the middle of the war.

130 How can someone so evil love his children like my parents love me?

Sometimes we think that someone who does evil things is *only* evil and mean. That's what we call a villain. In a play or movie or story, a villain is a character who is completely evil. When we see villains in stories we only see the evil they do. We never see that they have families that they love just like other people love their families.

In real life, no person is all good or all evil. We are all part good and part bad. Some people may choose to do good most of the time. They are usually called good people. Some people choose to do bad things most of the time, and they are called evil people. Even good people can do things that are very bad. Sometimes evil people can do things that are very good. We can never really know how much each person is good or evil; but we can tell whether the things they do are good or evil.

We are all born with what is called a conscience inside of us. A conscience is the feelings we get inside that let us know when the bad part of us wants to do something wrong. Sometimes we choose to do wrong things and then we feel guilty. Sometimes we choose to do right things and then we feel good. Can you remember when either of those things happened to you? Well, every person has that choice inside of them.

We see Saddam Hussein as a villain because he has done so many bad things that have been reported in the news. He has lied, cheated, stolen other people's things, tried to steal another country, and attacked and killed innocent people.

We also see him as a villain because when he does evil things, he does not agree that they are wrong. He acts like he can do whatever he wants and hurt whoever he wants, and even kill whoever he wants. When someone tries to convince people that evil is good, he is easily see as being evil. But remember, he does have good parts inside of them, and he usually shows that side to his family.

131 Why did Saddam Hussein want a new country when he already has one of his own?

No one can say for sure, but there are some reasons that seem to make sense. Saddam Hussein says that Kuwait belongs to Iraq because it was not fair the way the land was divided up in the first place. He thinks that Kuwait should have always been a part of Iraq.

Have you ever had to share a piece of cake with someone else and your mom or dad divided it for you? What happens if you don't think it was divided fairly? Do you sometimes wait until your mom or dad isn't looking and try to grab another piece for yourself to make it fair? Well, Saddam Hussein says that the land wasn't divided fairly, even though all the other nations thought it was. So he decided to try to grab it back.

Another reason could be that Saddam Hussein was jealous. There is a lot of oil in the ground in the Middle East. Oil is worth a lot of money, and whoever has the oil can do things to help their country and their people. They can even get a stronger army and then have even more power to do what they want. Iraq used to have a lot of oil and a lot of money from their oil, but they used up a lot of both their money and their oil to fight an eight-year war against Iran.

The people of Kuwait had a lot of oil and a lot of money. They didn't use their money to fight a war. They were using their money to take care of their people and to make their country a better place in which to live. They even used a lot of their money to help Iraq when they needed help during the war against Iran.

There are many more people in Iraq than there are in Kuwait. After the Iraqi government used most of their oil money to fight a war, they thought it wasn't fair that the people in Kuwait lived richer lives than the people in Iraq. The Iraqi leaders got jealous of this, and this could be part of the reason that they wanted to take over another country.

There is another reason some people think that Saddam Hussein wants Kuwait when he already has a country. When he was a younger man, before he was the leader of Iraq, he tried to kill Iraq's leader, the prime minister. He was sentenced to death and ran away to Egypt to hide. While he was hiding in Egypt, he was taught by a man named Gamal Abdel Nassar, who was president of Egypt at that time. This man believed that someone should create an independent Arab kingdom from the "Atlantic all the way to the Gulf." That area would include Kuwait and Saudi Arabia. Some people think that Saddam Hussein sees himself as the person to make this happen by taking control of his neighboring Arab countries.

132 Is it wrong to hate Saddam Hussein?

Hatred is a feeling. It is one of the strongest feelings we can have. We need to remember that feelings are not right or wrong, they just are there. So in that sense it is not wrong to hate Saddam Hussein.

Hatred is not a happy or comfortable feeling. If feelings could be described as pretty or ugly, hate would be an ugly feeling. We are not bad people just because we feel ugly feelings. Sometimes bad things happen, and it is natural for us to have some ugly feelings.

The Bible tells us that there is a time for everything. There is "a time to love; a time to hate" (Eccl. 3:8). It also says that we are to "love God and hate evil" (Ps. 97:10).

Saddam Hussein has done many evil things. It is not wrong to feel hatred of all the evil things that he has done. We need to try to remember, though, that hatred is an ugly emotion. If we only think about the hate inside, or if we hate other Arab people just because of Saddam Hussein, our attitudes can become ugly too. It's OK to feel all of our feelings, but we need to be careful not to let hatred make us forget the happy and pretty feelings too.

133 In the Persian Gulf War, what did we win?

In the Persian Gulf War, we won the battle to return Kuwait to its rightful owners. We also won a victory for freedom, to show the bullies of the world that they cannot just come in and take over a weaker nation, hurting whomever they want just because they are stronger.

We won the admiration and appreciation of all the people of Kuwait, the people of Saudi Arabia, and the other countries that were in the coalition. We also won the right to have some say about how the peaceful changes will be made in the world.

TWENTY
FAMILY
ACTIVITIES

Note to parents: These activities are offered as launching pads for discussion between you and your children; they don't substitute for your input. Use the activities to start talks with your children about war and peace. Some activities will help your children express their feelings; some will help them learn about warring countries; some will simply provide a context for your children to express thoughts and questions.

1. Have children draw a picture or cartoon of how they felt about the war. Then have them tell you about their picture.

2. Have a special family dinner made entirely of foods from one or more of the warring countries. You can even dress up as people from those countries. Or, prepare foods that the soldiers eat (from an army surplus store).

3. Dress up like the people in the warring countries, and take pictures of everyone dressed up. Or, have your kids make paper dolls of the people in the warring countries, including hats and clothes. Kids can learn about the dress and customs from newspaper or magazine photographs and encyclopedias.

4. Have your kids pretend that their stuffed animals or dolls are the warring countries. Clear the dining room table, pretend that it is the battlefield, and line up the dolls/stuffed animals against one another. Then ask your kids to explain why each side is fighting the other. This will help them understand why the war is going on and express their feelings about it.

5. Often kids are terrified of the weapons used in war. To help your children discuss and confront their fear, have them make a paper model of a weapon or piece of military hardware (rifle, jet, tank). Explain in basic terms what it does and probe their fears about it. Explain that God, who loves them, is bigger and mightier than all weapons.

6. Have your kids play hospital. They can put on makeup and pretend they're wounded, while others act as doctors and nurses. Or, have them play hospital using their stuffed animals or dolls, putting bandages on the wounds and talking about what combat and being wounded in combat is like.

7. Make a list of the capitals, chief imports and exports, population figures, and other key facts about the warring countries. Ask your kids to

guess these facts. Almanacs and encyclopedias are good sources for information.

8. Have your kids make flags of the countries
    involved in the war.

9. Have your kids make an American flag and
    display it somewhere in their rooms.

10. Buy an American flag for display outdoors,
    picked out by your kids. Have your kids
    help put it up and take it down each day.

11. Have your kids write, draw, or explain how
    they would have ended the war.

12. Have a scavenger hunt for war-related
    items. Give your kids a set amount of time
    to collect and gather all the items in and
    around the house that they can find. (These
    can include seemingly mundane items such
    as flashlights, water, jackets, flatware,
    glasses, and toy guns.)

13. Hold a pretend news conference with every
    person in the family participating. Don
    different hats and pretend to be various
    people — a general, a soldier, a housewife —
    and have your children pretend to be the
    reporters interviewing you. Wear different
    clothes each time you change identities.

14. Make a scrapbook about the war together with your children and piece it together over time. Be creative; your scrapbook could include:
    - pictures from newspapers and magazines
    - quotes from soldiers
    - miniature flags
    - appropriate Bible verses (any that are meaningful to you and/or your children, or ones you memorize during this time)
    - names and pictures of soldiers they see and hear about in the news. (This can also become a nightly prayer list, so you can pray for soldiers by name.)
    - samples of writing in the languages of the warring countries (English, Arabic, Russian, etc.)
    - other things about the war that mean something to your family

15. Make a puzzle out of a map. Cut out the warring countries and have your kids put the map back together. This can open discussion (for older kids) about the brokenness caused by sin in our world and who can put it back together.

16. If you or other close relatives served in previous wars, tell your children stories about some of those experiences.

17. Have your kids find the warring countries on a map or globe, and then find their own country. This can open discussion of how far away or close the war is.

18. Have your kids draw pictures of the kinds of people affected by the war — soldiers, moms and dads, and other children (pets are also affected). This can open discussion of who is affected by war and what needs war creates, including the need for hope in Christ.

19. Have everyone imagine that your family lives in the war zone. Ask your children what they might hear; what they might see. As a family, what would be different for you? What would you do differently? What would you have in your closets? In your kitchen? In the basement?

20. Read the Bible together. You can memorize verses, have your children read verses from cards each evening, or make a poster of a verse for their rooms. This book includes a list of verses appropriate for wartime.

CREATIVE THINGS TO DO FOR THE TROOPS

1. Write and send a card, letter, or a poem of encouragement or thanks to a soldier, an officer, or a government official.

2. Record and send a cassette letter.

3. Record and send a video.

4. Record and send a song or a rap. Sing it yourself or with others with or without instruments. Make your own instruments. Make up your own song or use a popular or patriotic one.

5. Send silly snapshot photographs or nice portraits. Have your picture taken four times in an instant photo booth. Make a homemade frame for a portrait. Send a flat, clear plastic, magnet-backed or key-chain photo holder with a picture. Remember to write a message and sign your name on the back of the photo.

6. Make up a story or book to send or keep. Just like a real one would look like. Do it individually or as a group. Add illustrations if you

want — draw your own or cut them out of magazines. Dedicate it to a service person.

7. Make and send a jigsaw puzzle picture or letter.

8. Make and send something fun or funny. A cartoon, comic, or joke, or send the comics section from your newspaper. Crosswords, word searches, and other puzzles can be entertaining. Anything that will result in a smile or laughter is a good morale-builder.

9. Make and send a banner, a poster, or a message out of large connected letters. Use cloth, felt, paper or other materials and decorations. The message letters could be connected by paper fasteners or use one whole piece of paper and accordion-fold it after each letter like a fan. Remember to provide tape or tacks and/or string to hang it up with.

10. Make and send a coat of arms. Put your family or group name, motto, symbol, and anything else for which your group stands for or believes in on it.

11. Make and send a flag. This could be of your country or your family or your particular kind of group. Design a symbol, select the colors,

consider a motto to put on it. Make it out of paper or cloth. Remember some way of hanging or waving it, such as a dowel rod slipped through a sturdy seam or some rope tied to or through some reinforced holes in the flag.

12. Make and maintain a ongoing scrapbook of events and activities. While a family member or friend is away, record memories, significant news, accomplishments, etc. for them to read about when they return.

13. Read, study, and talk about books, especially ones about feelings.

14. Try acting out a real or made-up story or play. Make it complete with costumes and props. Do it in front of others who might benefit from seeing it.

15. Set up your own military camp. Set up a tent indoors or outdoors and try living like a soldier does.

16. Make and send a care package. Contact Christian Military Fellowship (see the Resource appendix) for ideas of what to put in it.

17. Make and keep a "wish jar." Whenever you or another complains or expresses sorrow or

anger about the war or someone in it, you can try to turn it into a wish instead.

First, acknowledge the feeling and the reason behind it. Next, provide a constructive outlet for the feeling, such as a good cry or some physical activity. Also, give an encouraging response like a hug and some kind words. Then, in an effort to turn the experience around into something hopeful say something such as, "I wish . . . " or "Now, let's make a wish."

Get the wish written down on a piece of paper; have it signed and dated if desired. Fold it up and put it in the wish jar. At the end of the war, the entire group can read over their wishes or even guess whose wish was whose. A family member who was in the war will be able to see the many thoughts there were about them and their situation while they were gone. See how many wishes came true and be glad!

18. Make and keep a "thank-you box." This is similar to the "wish jar." Whenever you or another notices something good or feels grateful, say out loud, "I am thankful!" Write down what it is you or they are thinking of. Sign and date the piece of paper if desired. Fold it up and put it in the

"thank-you box." Whenever someone feels downcast, the messages can be reviewed to lift spirits and renew thoughts.

At the end of the week, a "thank-you fest" could occur by reading them aloud and a guessing game could be played to find out who wrote each message. There is always something to be thankful about even in what we think are the worst of times.

19. Set up an altar or memorial. Find a place for a center of worship and/or remembrance of loved ones, friends, and other people in the war. Put pictures, a candle to light, your "wish jar" and "thank-you box," a flag, ribbons, or anything else that has special meaning to you. Daily or weekly gather around this with the members of your family or classroom or group. Sing songs, share thoughts, and pray together.

20. Do something helpful and caring for others. It is good to get our minds off ourselves for a while and remember that others have needs and concerns too, besides what involves war.

    Here are some ideas for doing just that: Visit the elderly or the physically ill in your local nursing home or hospital. Adopt a pet.

Sponsor a needy child from a Third World country and write to him or her. (Contact Compassion International, The United Christian Children's Fund, or World Vision Childcare, for example.) Bring flowers or a plant to someone. Make a meal or a food item for somebody. Do a chore or errand for a friend—without being asked. Babysit for free.

21. Plan and put on a Homecoming/Victory Party and Parade. Use the creative things you have done already or the ideas listed earlier as decorations and program items. Have plenty of music, noisemakers, food, and fun available. Remember to record the event in photographs and on audio and video cassete tape if you can. Give a warm "welcome home" and "congratulations" to the service men and women. Celebrate the end of the war and their homecoming!

RESOURCES FOR FURTHER INFORMATION

American Academy of Pediatrics
141 N.W. Point Boulevard
P.O. Box 927
Elk Grove Village, IL 60009
708/228-5005
(Has a committee working on the issue.)

American Psychological Association
1200 17th Street, N.W.
Washington, D.C. 20036
202/955-7603
(Has published a Fact Sheet on children and war.)

Christian Military Fellowship
P.O. Box 36440
Denver, CO 80236
303/761-1959
(An Evangelical association providing spiritual, educational and personal support, and free literature to American military personnel and their families.)

The Compassionate Friends, Inc.
National Office
P.O. Box 3696
Oak Brook, IL 60522-3696
708/990-0010
(Therese Goodrich, Executive Director. A non-denominational network of local chapters which provide group support, education, a newsletter, and minimal cost publications to adult siblings and parents who have lost their children due to any cause of death. Does not serve spouses and children of deceased persons.)

Family Communications, Inc.
Attn: Hedda Sharapan
4802 Fifth Avenue
Pittsburgh, PA 15213
412/687-2990
(also known as Mister Rogers' Neighborhood)

Harvard Medical School
Attn: T. Berry Brazelton
25 Shattuck Street
Boston, MA 02115
617/432-1550

Military Family Resource Center
Attn: JanaLee Sponberg
Department of Defense
Office of Family Policy/Support
4015 Wilson Boulevard, Suite 903
Arlington, VA 22203 703/696-4555

Military Order of the World Wars (MOWW)
435 N. Lee Street
Alexandria, VA 22314
703/683-4911
(Lt. General C.M. Talbot, USAF (retired),
Executive Officer. An organization of 20,000
commissioned officers, flight officers, and
warrant officers who served on active duty in
the armed forces, the National Oceanographic
and Atmospheric Administration, and the United
States Public Health service since April 6, 1917.
Presents medals and awards to ROTC cadets;
promotes patriotic education in schools.)

MOWW, Operation Friendship
P.O. Box 661001, AMF OHIAP
Chicago, IL 60666-1001
(Aaron Kagann, Director and retired Air Force
captain. Illinois and Midwest chapters of
MOWW. Is sponsoring a nationwide
letter-writing campaign for the 475,000

American troops in the Persian Gulf until they are sent home. Please write if you wish to "adopt" a trooper and send him or her a letter once a week.)

National Association of School Psychologists
Department DS
8455 Colesville Road
Silver Spring, MD 20910
301/608-0500
(Has free pamphlet, "Tips for Teachers and Parents," plus a report, "Resources and Crisis Intervention," available for $22.00 payable by check in advance.)

National Childhood Grief Institute
3300 Edindorough Way
Edina, MN 55435
612/832-9286

National Health Information Clearinghouse
800/336-4797
(Health and Human Services Hotline)

National League of Families of American Prisoners and Missing in Southeast Asia
1001 Connecticut Avenue N.W., Suite 219
Washington, D.C. 20036
202/223-6846
24-hr information: 202/659-0133
(Ann Mills Griffiths, Executive Director. Seeks to: verify the status of servicepersons still listed as missing in action in Southeast Asia, secure the return of the remains of American servicepersons who died during the Viet Nam War, secure the release and return of all POWS; educate the public on all of these issues. Acts as liason between the families of POWs/MIAs and the United States government.)

Navigators
P.O. Box 6000
Colorado Springs, CO 80934
719/598-1212
(Worldwide evangelism and discipleship network to help military personnel apply Scripture to everyday life.)

Officer's Christian Fellowship
P.O. Box 1177
Englewood, CO 80150
303/761-1984
*(Paul Pettijohn, Executive Director. Evangelical
organization which ministers to the entire
military society worldwide—especially the
officer corps and including cadets and
midshipman. Provides literature, quarterly
magazine, book service, link-up service,
deployment packets, conference centers, lay
leader training seminars.)*

Overseas Christian Servicemen's Centers
P.O. Box 1268
Englewood, CO 80150
303/762-1400
*(Evangelism and discipleship ministry for
military personnel and their families.)*

PBS Video
"Kids Ask About War Guide"
1320 Braddock Place
Alexandria, VA 22314
703/739-5000

Project ME
Attn: Dennis D. Embry, Ph.D.
800 N. Swan, #114
Tucson, AZ 85711
602/322-9977
(Provides literature and individual and group counseling or sharing time)

The United States Department of Defense
— Air Force: 1-800/253-9276
— Army: 1-800/626-1440
— Coast Guard: 1-800/367-8724
— Marines: 1-800/523-2694
— Navy: 1-800/255-3808 (immediate family members) 1-800/732-1206 (other relatives and friends)
(Applies only to families of military personnel and civilians in the Persian Gulf; toll-free phone lines.)

State Department
Operations Center of Crisis Management
202/647-0900
(Applies only to families of civilians/private citizens in Gulf countries.)

TWENTY-FIVE BIBLE MEMORY VERSES

Some nations brag of armies and weapons. But our boast is in the Lord our God. Psalm 20:7

And so we need not be afraid. Not even if the world blows up. Not even if the mountains crumble into the sea. Psalm 47:2

He is not afraid of bad news. He does not live in fear of what may happen. For he is settled in his mind. He knows that the Lord will take care of him. Psalm 112:7

Just as water is turned into ditches, so the Lord directs the king's thoughts. He turns them wherever he wants to. Proverbs 21:1

The wicked will finally lose. The righteous will finally win. Proverbs 21:18

Go ahead and get ready for the conflict. But victory comes from God. Proverbs 21:31

Do not be happy when your enemy meets trouble. Let there be no gladness when he falls. Proverbs 24:17

The Lord will settle all fights between nations. All the nations will make their weapons of war into tools to be used for peace. Then at last all wars will stop. And all training for war will end.
Isaiah 2:4

From eternity to eternity I am God. No one can stand in the way of what I do.   Isaiah 43:13

Many good men die. The godly often die before their time. And no one seems to care or wonder why. No one seems to know that God is taking them away from evil days ahead. For the godly who die shall rest in peace.
Isaiah 57:1-2

"For I know the plans I have for you," says the Lord. "They are plans for good and not for evil. I want to give you a future and a hope."
Jeremiah 29:11

"Happy are those who work hard to bring peace. For they shall be called the sons of God."
Matthew 5:9

"Give him first place in your life. Live as he wants you to. Then he will give all these things to you as well. So don't be worried about tomorrow. God will take care of your tomorrow, too. Live one day at a time."   Matthew 6:33-34

"You will hear about wars beginning. But this alone does not mean I am coming. These must come, but the end is not yet." Matthew 24:6

"Glory to God in the highest Heaven!" they sang. "May there be peace on earth for all those who please him." Luke 2:14

"I am leaving you my peace! And the peace I give isn't like the peace the world gives. So don't be troubled or afraid." John 14:27

"I have told you all this so that you will have peace. Here on earth you will have many trials and sorrows. But cheer up, for I have overcome the world!" John 16:33

When others are happy, be happy with them. If they are sad, share their sadness. Romans 12:15

Don't argue with anyone. Be at peace with everyone as much as you can. Romans 12:18

These troubles are quite small and won't last very long. This short time of trouble will bring God's richest blessing upon us forever! 2 Corinthians 4:17-18

Don't worry about anything. Instead, pray about everything. Tell God your needs, and don't forget to thank him for his answers. Philippians 4:6

So support each other and build each other up, just as you are already doing.
1 Thessalonians 5:11

Always be joyful. Always keep on praying. No matter what happens, always be thankful. This is God's will for you who belong to Christ Jesus.
1 Thessalonians 5:16-18

Let God have all your worries and cares. He is always thinking about you and watching everything that concerns you. 1 Peter 5:7

I heard a loud shout from the throne. It was saying, "Look, the home of God is now among men. He will live with them and they will be his people. Yes, God himself will be among them. He will wipe away all tears from their eyes. There shall be no more death, sorrow, crying, or pain. All of that has gone forever."
Revelation 21:3-4

FAMILY DEVOTIONS FOR TIMES OF WAR

Note to parents: Here are seven 10-to-15-minute family devotions you can do with your children. You can do them before breakfast, after dinner, or any other time when you can get the family together. Adapt them for the age of your kids — for younger children, emphasize the activities; for older kids, emphasize the discussions and have them read the Bible passages.

1—The World's Falling Apart!

Excite. Make a puzzle out of a map. Cut out the countries in and near the war zone and have your kids put them back together.

Explore. Say something like: "Sometimes we can feel as if the world is falling apart, especially when we hear about bombs, fighting, and war. It's like the puzzle we just put together, except the pieces are all mixed up. The Bible says a lot about our crumbling world. Let's take a look at what it says." Read each of these Bible passages and discuss the questions that follow.

- Isaiah 43:13 — What does this verse tell us about God?

- Proverbs 21:1 — Today, kings would be the leaders of countries, like presidents and prime ministers. What does this verse teach about God and leaders?
- John 16:33 — What is Jesus telling his disciples about what they can expect in the world? Why should they cheer up?
- Romans 8:28 — What can God do with the bad things that happen in our world, like war?

Continue the discussion by asking: "What could we tell someone who is very afraid and sad because of what is happening in the world? (Hint: think of something you learned from the verses.)"

Explain. Compliment your kids on their answers, and then say something like: "The world is not falling apart. No matter what happens or how bad events seem, we know that God is in control. No matter what happens in the world, he can bring about good. This should give us hope and courage to live the way he wants and to depend on him."

Express. In your closing prayers together, encourage your kids to admit their feelings to God. It's OK to tell him when they feel afraid or nervous about what's going on. Then thank him for being in control and for giving us hope.

Exercise. Have everyone think about a friend who might be frightened or nervous about the war. Encourage everyone to tell their friends about God's control over events in the world.

Memorize John 16:33 together: "I have told you all this so that you will have peace. Here on earth you will have many trials and sorrows. But cheer up, for I have overcome the world!"

2—Who Cares?

Excite. Bring out a stuffed animal and pretend that it is the family pet. (Use a live pet if you have one.) Ask your kids what they would do to take good care of this pet.

Explore. Say something like: "Though we're not pets, we like to be taken care of just like they do. But it's easy to feel afraid and lonely when we hear about war and people fighting. We may even think that no one cares about us. The Bible tells us that God cares. Let's see what it says." Read these Bible verses aloud and then ask the questions that follow.

- Psalm 112:7
- Philippians 4:19
- 1 Peter 5:7

What do these verses tell us about God? What should we do because God loves and cares for us? Say something like: "God cares for us; he watches over us; he loves us. We can see evidence of his love all around us."

Hold up the following items and ask how each one shows God cares for us:
- food
- medicine
- money
- family pictures
- a Bible
- picture of a house
- something else:_____

Explain. Say: "Because we know God loves and cares for us, we don't have to be afraid. We can 'let God have all our worries' (1 Peter 5:7). When we hear bad news and begin to feel bad or lonely, we can pray and tell God how we feel."

Express. Pray by thanking God for his care and love. Encourage your children to tell him about any fears or worries they have.

Exercise. Make a poster that says, "God cares. — 1 Peter 5:7" that your kids can put beside their beds.

Memorize 1 Peter 5:7 together: Let God have all your worries and cares. He is always thinking about you and watching everything that concerns you.

3—What Can We Do?

Excite. Have your kids finish each of these "What if" sentences:

What would you do if . . .
- a parrot landed in the backyard?
- our uncle became president of the United States?
- a friend was feeling very sad?
- you became really hungry in the middle of the night?

Explore. Say something like: "Some of those situations are a little strange, but your answers were very good. If we use our imagination, we can think of what we might do in almost any situation. Sometimes we would like to help someone but the person seems too big or too far away from us. War is like that—we didn't start it, and everything seems to be beyond our control. But we would like to help if we can.

Let's use our imagination again: What could we do to help during this war?" Discuss this for a while.

The Bible gives us some ideas about how to help. Read these verses for ideas:
- 1 Thessalonians 5:11
- James 2:15-16
- James 5:16

Next, read the following phrases aloud and discuss the questions that follow.
- "Support each other and build each other up." (1 Thessalonians 5:11) How can we support or encourage our soldiers? (Send them letters, cookies, etc.) Who else could we encourage? (The president, elected officials, friends with relatives in the war, etc.)
- "If you don't give him clothes or food, what good does that do?" (James 2:15) During this time of war, who could use some clothes or food from us? (Relief agencies, families with wage-earners sent to fight that now need food or baby-sitting help, soldiers who would appreciate cookies, etc.)
- "Pray for each other." (James 5:16) Who needs our prayers? (Our elected officials, soldiers, people in war-torn countries, etc.)

What should we pray about? (Safety,
wisdom, that good will prevail,
healing, etc.)

Explain. Say: "As you can see, there are a lot of
things we can do about war. We're not as
helpless as we may have thought. We cannot
stop war, but we do know God, and he can do
anything. He has also given us hands and feet
and resources to use in Jesus' name."

Express. Make a prayer list together (including
people's names, needs, etc.) and pray for the
people and needs on the list.

Exercise. This week, pray about the people and
needs on your prayer list, and do one or more of
the other activities you brainstormed.

Memorize 1 Thessalonians 5:11 together: So
support each other and build each other up, just
as you are already doing.

4—What Does the Future Hold?

Excite. Have your kids draw a picture of "the
house of the future" and then talk about it.

Explore. Say: "Nobody knows exactly what the
future will be like. Some people even think we

have no future because of war. The Bible gives us some clues about what the future really holds."

Read aloud these Bible passages; then ask the question that follows.
- Matthew 24:6
- 1 Corinthians 15:52
- 2 Corinthians 4:17-18

What do these verses say is going to happen in the future?

Next, read aloud Jeremiah 29:11. Then discuss: What kind of plans does God have for us? How does this give us hope?

Explain. Say: "War has been around for a long time. And there will probably be wars for as long as the world exists. But God has plans for us, and nothing can stop those plans. The future for God's people is bright, not bleak."

Express. In your closing prayer, thank God for the future. Thank him for having plans for us and for not leaving us without hope.

Exercise. Have your kids draw another picture, this time reflecting their future as God has described it.

Memorize Jeremiah 29:11 together: "For I know the plans I have for you," says the Lord. "They are plans for good and not for evil. I want to give you a future and a hope."

5—Happy Are the Peacemakers

Excite. Have your kids pretend that their stuffed animals or dolls are the warring countries. Line up the animals opposite each other (in their battle positions) and explore what they're doing. Then have your kids hold a pretend peace conference. Each side must send a representative to talk about terms of peace. (Even if your kids don't know what to say, try the conference anyway.)

Explore. Say something like: "War seems to be easy to start. Everybody wants to fight about something, whether it be territory, claims, pride, or hatred. But peace is harder to achieve. Where does peace come from? The Bible talks about how important peacemakers are in the world. Let's see what it says." Read these verses and discuss the questions together.

- Matthew 5:9 — Who shall be called the sons of God? What kind of work can people do to bring peace?
- Luke 2:14 — Why did the angels appear to the shepherds? What was their message about peace?
- Psalm 68:30 — This is a prayer to God.

What is the writer asking God to do? Why might we call this writer a peacemaker?

- Isaiah 2:4 — How will lasting peace come about?

Discuss: Who are some of the peacemakers in the world today? What are they doing to bring about peace? What can we do to help bring about peace in the world?

Explain. Say: "War seems big and far away, run by people who have a lot more power than we have. But we can still help bring about peace. The most important thing we can do is pray. We can also encourage and support people trying to bring about peace."

Express. Pray for peace. Ask God to stop the fights between the nations and to bring about his will.

Exercise. Write a letter together as a family to a person of influence trying to bring about peace (an elected official, diplomat, etc.). Thank the person for his or her efforts.

Memorize Matthew 5:9 together: "Happy are those who work hard to bring peace. For they shall be called the sons of God."

6—Casualties of All Kinds

Excite. Gather around a globe or map of the world. Identify several countries that are at war or experiencing conflict.

Next, list the warring countries served by missionaries from your church or denomination. Have your kids tell whom they know in each of those countries.

Explore. Say: "It's easy to forget about the people affected by war because wars are often far away. But wars affect real people. We may even know some of the people being affected by war."

Read these Bible passages aloud and discuss the questions:

- Proverbs 24:17 — Why do you think we shouldn't be glad when our enemy meets trouble?
- Luke 10:30-37 — The Samaritans and Jews were usually enemies. But here the Samaritan man went out of his way to help the Jewish man who had been robbed and hurt by thieves. Why do you think the Samaritan man stopped to help?

Next, discuss these questions:

- Who gets hurt in a war? In what ways are people hurt?

- Many countries are enemies of our country, with leaders saying harsh words back and forth to each other. What should be our attitude be toward the people who live in "enemy" countries? How are missionaries and other Christians in "enemy" countries like the good Samaritan?
- What can we do to encourage and help people whom we know living in warring countries?

Explain. Say: "When we see people in other countries, such as mothers and children and innocent civilians, hurt by wars, then we realize that 'enemy' countries aren't just bad guys. Every country has people just like us. Also, there are Christians in every country of the world; that's like having part of our family there."

Express. Pray for people being hurt by war.

Exercise. Write a letter to a missionary family you know in a warring country (if possible, write to a family with children similar in age to your own).

Memorize Romans 12:15 together: "When others are happy, be happy with them. If they are sad, share their sadness."

7—On the Home Front

Excite. Ask your children: "What don't you like about _____?" (Fill in the blank with the name of someone your kids don't get along with.)

Or, ask specific questions about a recent conflict that your kids had. For example, you could ask: "Why were you and _____ arguing? What caused the fight between you and _____?"

Explore. Say: "Wars seem far away, but they're also close to home. We fight with words and other weapons instead of tanks and guns. So in some ways we have our own personal wars. Let's see what the Bible says about how we should treat people we don't get along with."

Read these Bible verses together and discuss the questions after each:
- Psalm 34:14 — What will it take for us to "live in peace" with people?
- Matthew 5:43-47 — Who are our personal enemies? How are we supposed to treat them?
- Romans 12:18 — What can we do to make peace in our relationships? What can we do to avoid or stop arguments?

Referring back to some of the conflicts already discussed, ask what you and your kids can do to make peace in those situations.

Explain. Say: "We talk a lot about peace in the world. But we can make peace right here at home. As we read in the Bible, we can be 'peacemakers' by trying hard to be at peace with everyone, and even to be kind to those we don't get along with. We can't control how people act toward us, but we can control how we act toward them—we can treat them kindly, refuse to fight with them, and pray for them."

Express. Pray for the people with whom you and your kids don't get along well. Also pray that you all will be able to make peace with "difficult people" as much as possible.

Exercise. Brainstorm one kind act each of you could do toward someone you don't like. (Ideas: send a card, say hello, offer to help, invite to a church activity, etc.)

Memorize Romans 12:18 together: "Don't argue with anyone. Be at peace with everyone as much as you can."

A CHILDREN'S GLOSSARY

aircraft carrier: A huge ship that has an airstrip and carries aircraft while at sea.

air attack: Air raid. When fighting airplanes fly overhead and shoot at things on the ground.

air force: The part of a country's armed forces trained to fight using aircraft.

ally: A person or country who is friendly with you and shares some of the same thoughts, feelings, and actions as you.

Allied forces: The soldiers of countries who are allies during a war like France, Great Britain, Italy, and America.

basic training: The first eight weeks of soldier school.

barbed wire: Wire with sharp points called *barbs* coming out of it. It is used in fences and will cut and hurt when touched.

bomb: 1. (noun) A hollow case filled with something that can explode. It is used as a weapon. It explodes when it hits something or when it is set off by a fuse or a timing device. 2. (verb) To throw or drop a bomb on.

bombard: To attack with bombs or heavy fire from big guns.

bomber: An airplane that can drop bombs.

bunker: A place of protection dug into the ground and held in place with concrete or rocks and/or wood on or near a battlefield. A place to hide in and shoot from.

camp: A place for one or more people to live outdoors for a time often in tents.

captain: The leader of a group.

Chief of Staff: The commanding officer of the army or air force and a member of the Joint Chiefs of Staff. One who is the main adviser to a commander in the armed forces.

civilian: A person who is not in the armed forces.

Communist: A person who believes in a way of life in which property and things that are sold — to be used by people — are owned by the government and are to be shared equally by all the people.

enemy: A person who fights you or starts a war.

enlist: 1. To get the help or support of someone or something. 2. To join or talk someone into joining the armed forces.

flag: A sign made of cloth. Each country in the world has one specially made that looks like no other one.

gas mask: A covering worn over the head. It has a filter to keep a person from breathing in poisonous gases (like mustard gas and nerve gas) and liquids through their nose and mouth.

government: The group of people who take care of the things and people of a certain place; who make rules and punish those who don't follow them; who are picked by the people to do this kind of work.

guard: A person who takes care of something or someone to keep it from being hurt or taken away.

helicopter: A machine that lifts off the ground and flies by blades (long sticks) that spin around very fast.

hostage: A person who is held as a prisoner until money is paid or promises are kept.

Islam: The religion of Moslems

invade: 1. To enter a place to take over the land, people, and everything there is for oneself or one's group or country. 2. To take away someone else's freedom and rights without them saying that is OK.

jet: A plane that flies very, very fast in the air.

jihad: Moslem term for a holy war.

military: 1. Having to do with the armed forces, soldiers, or war. 2. The army, navy, air force, and marine branches of the armed forces as a whole.

mine: A bomb that is put underground or underwater.

Missing in Action (MIA): A soldier that no one can find or that no one knows what happened to after a battle.

missile: Anything thrown or shot through the air.

missile launcher: A platform on the ground that pushes a missile or bomb into the air toward a target.

mobile: Able to be moved from place to place.

MRM: Meals-ready-made; the food soldiers carry with them to eat during a war.

Muslim: A person who believes in, worships, and obeys a god called Allah.

Operation Desert Shield: The name of the Allies' plan to put troops in Saudi Arabia to protect the people and oil fields there from possible attack by Iraq. A part of the Persian Gulf War of 1990-91.

Operation Desert Storm: The name of the Allies' plan to attack Iraqi troops in Kuwait and Iraq in order to make them leave the country of Kuwait. A part of the Persian Gulf War of 1990-91.

parachute: A large, round piece of cloth which people jump out of planes with so they can float slowly down to the ground. It attaches to your back in a pack and unfolds when you pull a string. The air fills it up like a balloon.

paratroopers: Soldiers who parachute out of planes to go fight in a war.

patriot: A person who loves his or her country and defends or supports it.

Patriot missile: A missile from the army of the United States that shoots down other missiles from the enemy.

patriotism: Love and loyal support of one's country. A sense of pride in the land or country of one's birth or citizenship.

The Pentagon: A five-sided, government building in Arlington, Virginia. Most of the offices of the United States Defense Department are here. The work of protecting what is important to the country is done here.

pilot: The person who flies an aircraft. The co-pilot is the person who helps the pilot fly an aircraft.

poison gas: Air that has something in it that makes you very sick and could even make you die if you breathe it.

president: The person who is the leader and most important person of a government; he or she decides what his or her country's people will do.

Prisoner of War (POW): A person who is found and caught by his or her enemy and put in prison during a war.

recruit: 1. A newly enlisted soldier or sailor. 2. A new member of any group or organization.

retreat: To back away from; to leave; to turn around and go the other way.

sanctions: Things done to someone or their country to make them obey the law — like keeping things they want and need away from them.

SCUD missile: A missile from the army of Iraq. It rushes forward in the air.

sortie: 1. A sudden attack of troops from a defensive position against the enemy. 2. One mission or attack by a single plane. 3. Raid.

submarine: "Under the sea;" a boat that can move under water and shoot underwater bombs called torpedoes.

surrender: To give up; to stop fighting.

tank: An enclosed, armored vehicle used in war. It moves on wheels with two long belts. It has machine guns and a cannon on it. People drive and ride inside it over land.

target: A person, place, or thing that is picked out and found to shoot at or blow up.

terrorist: A person who does things to scare, hurt, or kill innocent people just so he can get what he wants when he wants it.

trench: A long, narrow ditch in the ground. Soldiers use it to fight from.

troop: A group of persons doing something together, such as soldiers.

United Nations: An international organization made up of most of the countries of the world as its members. It was founded in 1945 to keep world peace. Its headquarters are in New York City in the United States.

weapon: Something used to fight with, to keep someone away from you, or to hurt or kill with.

withdraw: Leave; get out.

Peace on Earth

"Peace on Earth" was chosen as an anthem for The United Nation's International Year of Peace in 1986. Canadian Christian recording artist, Elaine Stacey, was part of the "Peace Choir," which was made up of representatives from more than eighty nations and participants of the 1986 World Exposition. In 1991, the song was re-recorded and videotaped featuring Elaine Stacey and an international choir of children made up of many who had family members serving in the Gulf War. This anthem of peace stirs hearts once again to pray that someday peace in our world will truly become more than just a dream.

Every night, I kiss my children.
Then, holding hands we pray,
"Lord, thank you for your goodness
And for another day.
Deliver us from evil
And help us, Lord, to see
In loving one another
We are also loving Thee."

And as I turn to leave them
A young voice softly speaks,
"Mom, there's war . . . people are dying.
Shouldn't we pray for peace?"
I kneel again beside them
And we each close our eyes.
Lord, in the hearts of children
The answer surely lies. . . .

Chorus 1:
Peace on earth.
Let it be

More than just a dream.
Every land from sea to sea
Living in harmony.

Chorus 2:
Peace on earth.
Let it be
While we still have time
To hear the children laugh and sing,
To lift our voices high.

Chorus 3:
It can start with you and me.
Hand in hand the world will see.
Though we live so far apart,
There's no distance heart to heart.

Repeat chorus 1
Repeat chorus 3
Repeat chorus 2

Every land from sea to sea
Livng in harmony.
Peace on earth.
"People, living all around the world,
Lift your voices to God in heaven.
Love's the answer,
We can make it work.
Pray for peace,
We can see it happen."

Written by Bruce W. Stacey, © 1991 Chelsea Road Productions

S P E C I A L   O F F E R

Song of Ages by Elaine Stacey. Cassette/Compact Disc
Canadian performing artist Elaine Stacey presents an
outstanding solo recording debut! Features the original
"Peace on Earth" recording and nine additional
original songs of Christian faith and hope that will
move and challenge every listener. Elaine, one of
Canada's leading Christian artists, presents her first
international release on this superbly crafted album
which highlights her warm and distinctive vocal style.
Elaine Stacey - "Song of Ages"
Digitally Mastered Chrome Cassette - $6.00
Compact Disc - $10.00
(Please include $1.50 for postage and handling with
each order.)

To Order Write:
Crossroads U.S.A.
Crossroads Christian Communications, Inc.
Box 486
Niagara Falls, NY 14302

Enclose your name, address and check or money order.
Please allow 6-8 weeks for delivery.